IMPORTANT THINGS THAT REALLY MATTER

Sharing a life-time of study and experience

DARL E. ARBOGAST

IMPORTANT THINGS THAT REALLY MATTER

International Standard Book Number 0-87012-875-2
Library of Congress Control Number 2016920327
Printed in the United States of America
Copyright © 2016 by Darl E. Arbogast
Newport, Tennessee
All Rights Reserved
2016

Printed by
McClain Printing Company
Parsons, West Virginia
www.mcclainprinting.com
2016

ACKNOWLEDGMENTS

A special thanks to Kim Murphy, our local librarian, taking the time out of her busy schedule to proof my book.

I can't possibly mention all the people who have been a positive influence to me in my life.

I believe the results of the efforts of many, many people are evident in my life and what I have become or better said, who I have become.

First of all I give thanks to my dear precious mother, always encouraging me and giving me the right advice. She said many times that I could ask more questions than a Philadelphia lawyer; that was before I knew what a Philadelphia lawyer is or was, so I took it as a compliment.

I shall always remember Maxine Morrison, my first grade school teacher. She taught me to read, write, and understand math and some history. Her classroom started with a morning prayer, then all twenty children recited along with the pledge of allegiance to the American flag.

In her school we learned our lessons together, we prayed together, sang songs together and we played together in the school yard.

I believe children experiencing these activities together in their formative years have a great value.

During these years is where I learned the things I have based my life upon.

I also owe a debt of gratitude to our minister, Bill Angel who had a lot of influence on me and was responsible in encouraging me to read the Bible every day.

Some of the local men who attended our little Farmers Chapel Church near Kerens, West Virginia, also had a huge amount of influence on me. Men like Jack Morrison, George Lloyd, and Henry Bright. These men have long ago gone to their rest but their memory along with a lot of others in the community still lingers in my mind.

My first book was written in 2015 "Precious Memories" and was dedicated in memory to my dear precious mother, Gertie Ellen Teter-Arbogast.

My dad taught me many things too, he was named after the statesman, Henry Clay. Dad had grown up with the basic skills of farming and cutting timber which he learned to love. He followed this life style and passed it on to his seven sons. He was also a firm believer in the work ethic and he made sure all of his sons received a healthy exposure to many skills relating to farm and timber skills.

When I was eight years of age, being the oldest son, dad took me to the woods and began training me to saw with a crosscut saw. Chainsaws had not been invented yet.

IMPORTANT THINGS THAT REALLY MATTER

Spending time with my dad our conversations lead to the importance of hard work, honest work and being fair to everyone.

Not only was my dad a good example, but when he gave me an assigned chore to do or other jobs I always did my best to try and please him and most of the time I was successful.

However, when I announced to the family that I was going to go on to high school a look of panic came over my dad's face. He realized he was losing a farmhand. I assured him I could hold up my end of the duties given to me at home and still go to school, and I did.

The exposure I had working with him, being trained on how to do things like cut hay with a team of horses, cut and skid logs, build and mend fences, and all the rest that goes into living on a farm have given me the balance I needed in raising my own family. I raised my children by the homesteader life style.

Last but not least, I must acknowledge my wife, Marilyn, who has been at my side all the way as I compiled and put all the pieces of my book together. She has served many tasks in making this book possible, things I probably never thought about. Without her I could not possibly have written this book, so thank you Marilyn for making all of this possible.

Darl E. Arbogast -

IMPORTANT THINGS THAT REALLY MATTER

IMPORTANT THINGS THAT REALLY MATTER

CHAPTER ONE
Important Things That Really Matter   1
What Really Matters   2

CHAPTER TWO
The Godhead   5
The Ten Commandments   6

CHAPTER THREE
How America Fell from Grace   17
The Early American Settlers Fought the Native Americans   18
Listing the Indian Wars   19

CHAPTER FOUR
Israel Migrating   21

CHAPTER FIVE
Sabbath Comes to Newport   27
What Went Wrong   29

CHAPTER SIX
Regulating Society   32

CHAPTER SEVEN
Obama's History   35
Mentoring with the Devil   38

CHAPTER EIGHT
American English   61

CHAPTER NINE
The Royal Line and the Priesthood   68
Chart   69

CHAPTER TEN
The Genealogy of Jesus	70
The Priesthood of Jesus Christ	73
Tithing	74

CHAPTER ELEVEN
True Womanhood Really Matters	78
Has True Womanhood Been Lost?	78
Why Woman Was Created	79
Women Have Questions, God Has the Answers	81
The Ultimate Goal	84

CHAPTER TWELVE
Are Men Fulfilling Their Responsibilities?	94

CHAPTER THIRTEEN
Successful Child Rearing	104
School Shootings	106
Childhood Accidents	107
Diseases of Baby's First Year	110
Tobacco	113

CHAPTER FOURTEEN
Abortion	116
America Doomed?	118

CHAPTER FIFTEEN
People of a Nation	125

CHAPTER SIXTEEN
Christianity Begins	131

IMPORTANT THINGS THAT REALLY MATTER

CHAPTER SEVENTEEN
Love a Splendid Thing   134

CHAPTER EIGHTEEN
The Importance of Proper Food   138

CHAPTER NINETEEN
The Power of Positive Reading   151

CHAPTER TWENTY
What is Heaven   159
What Happens When We Die   165
The False Trinity   166

CHAPTER TWENTY ONE
The Reward of the Saved   168

CHAPTER TWENTY TWO
Millennium Temple   174

CHAPTER TWENTY THREE
Ancient Israel Resurrection   178

CHAPTER TWENTY FOUR
Important Christian Things That Really Matter   181
Holy Days   184
Holy Days or Holidays   192

CHAPTER TWENTY FIVE
The Paradise of God   196

CHAPTER TWENTY SIX
Conclusion   202

IMPORTANT THINGS THAT REALLY MATTER

IMPORTANT THINGS THAT REALLY MATTER

by Darl E. Arbogast

INTRO: Charles Krauthammer once wrote a book chronicling three decades of what he believed were things that matter.

Some things noted by him that matter are lives of the good and the great, the innocence of dogs, the cunning of cats, the elegance of nature, the wonders of space, the difference between historical guilt and historical responsibility, homage and sacrilege in monumental architecture, plus other subjects.

Charles Krauthammer covered topics such as manners, pride and prejudices, follies, passions and pastimes, heaven and earth, citizen and state, conundrums, body and soul, man and God, memory and monuments.

He also covered Zionism and the fate of the Jews, the golden age of the 1980's and 1990's, then the age of unholy terror, bombing the World Trade Center, the rise of fanatical Islam, leadership and the absence thereof particularly in America under Obama.

Then he surmised about the age to come: "Hyperinflation", "Death by drones", and "No hiding from history".

He winds down in his book with four essays on "America and the World", "The Unipolar Moment" (1990), "Democratic Realism" (2004) and "Decline is a Choice" (2009).

He ends his book with Obama and the Arc of history picturing the president as a bewildered bystander and rightly so. Obama has behaved like a dawdling adolescent who has not a clue as to how to lead a country, a man with a teenage mind living in a fantasy world.

However in the view of many people, Obama as a Muslim at HEART, perhaps is practicing in private. He apparently believes Muslims have always gotten a raw deal and he wants to help them with America's money.

The great minds of the world will take a different view of what really matters to the average person. For example: The average person does not care who, or how they discovered $E=mc^2$.

WHAT REALLY MATTERS

The big question is are all things really relative? Take into consideration things of science, chemistry, biology, mathematics, medicine, philosophy and religion.

Then consider the sub-terranean, the topography of the landscape, the immeasurable air mass enveloping the earth, the solar system, sun, moon, stars, high tide and low tide all of which are predictable.

Also consider how the planets follow a non-collision course laid out mathematically and they travel in their orbit at a certain speed. Halley's Comet for centuries was thought to be an omen but now it is regarded to be proof of a deep harmony among the planets.

Halley's Comet is a mass of rock and ice a few miles wide caught in a kind of vortex making an endless revolution around our sun. This comet is far enough from the sun to keep it from melting and its orbit brings it close enough to the earth for us to see it move across the sky. It then travels 3 billion miles away from earth only to return again exactly 75 years later. This comet is always right on time as it displays its light for all the people on the earth to see.

If by chance we witnessed its flight in 1986 we may not live long enough to see it again in 2061.

Mark Twain was rather proud in saying he came in with Halley's Comet and would go out with it.

Another question to consider regarding the discussion of laws is that God has fixed in place certain irrefutable laws that run on automatic, they continue to do what they were designed to do when the Lord God set these things in motion. God created many things many centuries ago, long before the first man and woman walked upon the earth and they will continue in their assigned duties on into the future even if mankind were to eliminate all physical life from planet earth; their existence is not predicated on our existence.

In the face of all these things what should take top priority? Perhaps such things as: "Law and order, justice, mercy, faith, and love", these are the important things that really matter!

The upper level of law is of course divine law. We can not have divine law without first having a Divine Being. Neither can you have order without law. Laws are spoken and written and established, this is why the universe runs like a clock, as it is the order established by divine law.

It is Divine Law which affects mathematical law and chemistry law and all phases of physical law. The laws that govern our society were taken from the divine law as written down by Moses and spoken by God.

If mankind were to wipe the earth clean of human existence the sun would still come up every morning and go down in the evening, time would pass unnoticed but it would still pass. The Halley's Comet would still visit every 75 years, right on time, unnoticed and unappreciated, spring would turn to summer, summer to autumn and autumn to winter with no one to note it, paint it or appreciate it or make a photograph.

Certain laws of nature are just that, they are certain and they react to a built in design so they need nothing from mankind to continue on to infinity.

CHAPTER TWO

THE GODHEAD

The first duty of man that really matters is to recognize and admit that there would be no creation without a Creator. Some of the biblical writers referred to the Divinity as a Godhead.

Romans 1:20 thru 22 NKJ - [20] For since the creation of the world His invisible *attributes* are clearly seen, being understood by the things that are made, *even* His eternal power and Godhead, so that they are without excuse, [21] because, although they knew God, they did not glorify *Him* as God, nor were thankful, but became futile in their thoughts, and their foolish hearts were darkened. [22] Professing to be wise, they became fools.

Colossians 2:9, 10 NKJ - [9] For in Him dwells all the fullness of the Godhead bodily; [10] and you are complete in Him, who is the head of all principality and power.

A Godhead implies there exists more than one divine being, there are two in the Godhead as written in John 1:1 thru 5 NKJ - [1] In the beginning was the Word, and the Word was with God, and the Word was God. [2] He was in the beginning with God. [3] All things were made through Him, and without Him nothing was made that was made. [4] In Him was life, and the life was the light of men. [5] And the light shines in the darkness, and the darkness did not comprehend it. (The Creator became Jesus Christ, the Spokesman of the Godhead.)

The Bible reveals one divine being to be the MOST HIGH GOD and the other to be the Creator of all things, who became Jesus Christ. The Godhead's power, force and energy is called the Holy Spirit (pneuma in Greek).

Biblical scholars have placed the earth's creation at 4000 B.C. It was nearly 1400 B.C. before the written law was given to mankind by the Creator through Moses. The outline of the law is called the "Ten Commandments". The "Ten Commandments" are written in two places in the Holy Bible. Exodus 20:1 thru 17 and Deuteronomy 5:6 thru 21.

THE "TEN COMMANDMENTS"

Exodus 20:1 thru 17 NKJ - **1** And God spoke all these words, saying: **2** "I *am* the Lord your God, who brought you out of the land of Egypt, out of the house of bondage. **3** You shall have no other gods before Me. **4** "You shall not make for yourself a carved image, or any likeness *of anything* that *is* in heaven above, or that *is* in the earth beneath, or that *is* in the water under the earth; **5** you shall not bow down to them nor serve them. For I, the Lord your God, *am* a jealous God, visiting the iniquity of the fathers on the children to the third and fourth *generations* of those who hate Me, **6** but showing mercy to thousands, to those who love Me and keep My commandments. **7** "You shall not take the name of the Lord your God in vain, for the Lord will not hold *him* guiltless who takes His name in vain. **8** "Remember the Sabbath day, to keep it holy. **9** Six days you shall labor and do all your work, **10** but the seventh day *is* the Sabbath of the Lord your God. *In it* you shall do no work: you, nor your son, nor your daughter, nor your male servant, nor your female servant, nor your cattle, nor your stranger who *is* within your gates. **11** For *in* six days the Lord made the heavens and the earth, the sea, and all that *is* in them, and rested the seventh day. Therefore the Lord blessed the Sabbath day and hallowed it. **12** "Honor your father and your mother, that your days may be long upon the land which the Lord your God is giving you. **13** "You shall not murder. **14** "You shall not commit adultery. **15** "You shall not steal. **16** "You shall not bear false witness against your neighbor. **17** "You shall not covet your neighbor's house; you shall not covet your neighbor's wife, nor his male servant, nor his female servant, nor his ox, nor his donkey, nor anything that *is* your neighbor's."

The Ten Commandments are the laws of the Creator etched in stone by the finger of God, Exodus 31:18 NKJ - **18** And when He had made an end of speaking with him on Mount Sinai, He gave Moses two tablets of the Testimony, tablets of stone, written with the finger of God.

Since these are God's laws and God is love the first four of these laws are instructions to mankind on how to return love to our Creator.

1 John 4:8, 16 NKJ - **8** He who does not love does not know God, for God is love. **16** And we have known and believed the love that God has for us. God is love, and he who abides in love abides in God, and God in him.

The fifth commandment has a double application in that it covers our earthly parents and our Heavenly Father. Do you want your days to be long upon the land the Lord has given to you? God tells us how in commandment number five!

Exodus 20:12 NKJ - **12** "Honor your father and your mother, that your days may be long upon the land which the Lord your God is giving you.

Matthew 15:4 NKJ – (Jesus said), **4 For God commanded, saying, 'Honor your father and your mother'; and, 'He who curses father or mother, let him be put to death.'**

The Apostle Paul wrote a whole chapter on the subject of love, it is 1 Corinthians 13. Read it as this is one of the <u>chief</u> things that really matters. It could change your life for the better and forever.

1 Corinthians 13:1 thru 13 NKJ - **1** Though I speak with the tongues of men and of angels, but have not love, I have become sounding brass or a clanging cymbal. **2** And though I have the gift of prophecy, and understand all mysteries and all knowledge, and though I have all faith, so that I could remove mountains, but have not love, I am nothing. **3** And though I bestow all my goods to feed the poor, and though I give my body to be burned, but have not

love, it profits me nothing. **4** Love suffers long and is kind; love does not envy; love does not parade itself, is not puffed up; **5** does not behave rudely, does not seek its own, is not provoked, thinks no evil; **6** does not rejoice in iniquity, but rejoices in the truth; **7** bears all things, believes all things, hopes all things, endures all things. **8** Love never fails. But whether there are prophecies, they will fail; whether there are tongues, they will cease; whether there is knowledge, it will vanish away. **9** For we know in part and we prophesy in part. **10** But when that which is perfect has come, then that which is in part will be done away. **11** When I was a child, I spoke as a child, I understood as a child, I thought as a child; but when I became a man, I put away childish things. **12** For now we see in a mirror, dimly, but then face to face. Now I know in part, but then I shall know just as I also am known. **13** And now abide faith, hope, love, these three; but the greatest of these is love.

As we understand there is an upper level of law. There is also an upper level of love from the same source and there is interaction between the two, this is not widely understood by many people today. Love is the fulfillment of the law Romans 13:10 NKJ - **10** Love does no harm to a neighbor; therefore love *is* the fulfillment of the law.

In the Old Testament the verb 'aḥ'āb means to love or to like and appears 250 times. First of all this word refers to the love a man has for a woman and visa-versa as a desire to mate within the bounds of matrimony. 'Aḥ'āb describes the emotional attachment.

This word, 'aḥ'āb is also used as love between parents and children as in Genesis 22:2 NKJ - **2** Then He (the Lord) said, "Take now your son, your only *son* Isaac, whom you love (describing Abraham's special attachment to his son Isaac), and go to the land of Moriah, and offer him there as a burnt offering on one of the mountains of which I shall tell you."

'Aḥ'āb is again used to describe the love Israel had for King David in 1 Samuel 18:16 NKJ - **16** But all Israel and Judah loved David, because he went out and came in before them. David was adored by them with deep admiration and total loyalty.

When the word Ahab picks up a suffix, used as a noun it has a different meaning; it appears 55 times in the Old Testament. This first usage is in Genesis 29:20 NKJ - **20** So Jacob served seven years for Rachel, and they seemed *only* a few days to him because of the love "ahabah" he had for her. It is used here in the sense of a general concept dealing with marital love which entails all aspects of that relationship, emotional and physical.

Jacob had a deep longing for Rachel but he was one who played by the rules and he is now recognized as the progenitor of many billions of people. Rachel gave him two sons (Joseph and Benjamin) and look at how their lives really mattered, not only to Israel but many-many people down through the centuries. We know Joseph really mattered to the Lord because He had it written down for us to read; he was morally upright like Jacob his father.

The word ḥāsīd which is an adjective describes a <u>godly person</u>, pious, devout and faithful, Psalms 12:1 NKJ - **1** To the Chief Musician. On an eight-stringed harp. A Psalm of David. Help, LORD, for the <u>godly man</u> ceases! For the faithful disappear from among the sons of men. (The word ḥāsīd does not rise to the level of saint it refers to moral, natural goodness; meek by nature.)

In the New Testament the highest level of love described is agapaō when used as a verb and agape' when used as a noun. Agapaō is top level love emitted from the Godhead; from the MOST HIGH – God the Father to His Son, Jesus Christ and returned; it is first of all emitted from the Father. Agape' is the primary source by which grace is extended to those God is calling to repentance.

The greatest and at the very highest of God's level of love is the relationship between God and His Son and their relationship with the human race in general; and to the converted Christians in their relationship with each other. Nothing expresses or compares with what we have witnessed and experienced in the gift of God's Son being sacrificed for our salvation; this is agape' in motion which is agapaō.

We must understand that this is not an impulse of our feelings, it is much higher than human emotion. This love is the outpouring concern of our Heavenly Father for His children and is shared by Christians for one another. John 15:13 NKJ – Jesus said, **13 Greater love has no one than this, than to lay down one's life for his friends.**

The human level of love is mostly of emotion, affection mainly, called "phileo". This love is between family members and close friends. Jesus used phileo some in regard to His disciples; as He was teaching them about the higher level of love.

In John 21:15 thru 17 NKJ - **15** So when they had eaten breakfast, Jesus said to Simon Peter, **"Simon, *son* of Jonah, do you** (agapaō**) love Me more than these?"** **16** He said to him again a second time, **"Simon, *son* of Jonah, do you love** (agapaō) **Me?"** **17** He said to him the third time, **"Simon, *son* of Jonah, do you love** (phileo) **Me?"**

This was the third time Jesus showed Himself to His disciples after His resurrection. Jesus asked Peter twice if he was loving Him on a spirit level! Then the third time He asked Peter if he loved Him as a brother. Peter answered in the affirmative each time.

Mark 12:31 NKJ – (Jesus said), **31 And the second, like *it, is* this: 'You shall love your neighbor as yourself.' There is no other commandment greater than these."**

The last five of the Ten Commandments are our instructions on how to love our fellowman on both the agape' and phileo levels.

Exodus 20:13 thru 17 NKJ - **13** "You shall not murder. **14** "You shall not commit adultery. **15** "You shall not steal. **16** "You shall not bear false witness against your neighbor. **17** "You shall not covet your neighbor's house; "You shall not covet your neighbor's wife, nor his male servant, nor his female servant, nor his ox, nor his donkey, nor anything that *is* your neighbor's."

Today we live in a fast paced technology driven world where the economy is the principle thing. We have worldwide trade moving back and forth, planes in the sky by the thousands, trains on the tracks, ships on the ocean, automobiles running to and fro day and night, trucks on the highways and on it goes.

We are scrambling today to do more, get more and have more.

The possessions and the things we have or what we want become the gods to our lives! A question we must ask ourselves is "Does it really matter to God as to who or what our god is"? The answer is emphatically yes, it really does matter! Many are falling into the same state of mind as the ancient Greeks. When people live in a fantasy world, looking for happiness and success in acquiring wealth and worldly goods they tend to make idols; fantasy gods of wood, hay, stone or some other material and some try to make God conform to the image they have of Him.

This is exactly as the ancient pagan Greeks did as they had more pagan icons, more images, more than you could count all contrived through fantasy and Zeus was the king of all their imaginary gods.

If we claim today to be Christian and downplay parts of the Bible so that it conforms to our lives and religious customs we are no better than those pagan

Greeks. To be like the pagans is absolutely futile, we must conform to God's Word, His way of life and in the process we will be transformed into His character image and become truly Christian because this will lead us through the process of repentance and conversion.

The goal of every Christian is to live an abundant happy life, a life of service and goodwill conforming to the very principles and ideals lived by Jesus Christ. It was He who gave the Ten Commandments to Moses. The last six commandments are instructions for how to love and respect our neighbors beginning at home.

These commandments are living laws and they apply equally in our homes, communities, states, countries and nations. They are laws that work when they are applied and obeyed. They are the true expression of love. Jesus said, "Love your neighbor as yourself."

We can readily ascertain how things like honor, fairness, loyalty, honesty, and respect for other people and their property promotes good relations between people beginning at home and being extended out to communities and all people on earth.

In today's world people who practice these laws are often taken advantage of and become victims of charlatans, shysters, thieves, swindlers, and others. However Jesus gave clear instructions on how to avoid falling victim to chicanery such as this.

Matthew 10:16 NKJ - (Jesus said), **16 "Behold, I send you out as sheep in the midst of wolves.**

Therefore be wise as serpents and harmless as doves".

Jesus had the ability to call fire down from heaven and consume his tormentors or He could speak the word and their breath would depart from them. He did not resort to either of these tactics as He was more interested in the deep things of God, things that really do matter; shaking off a pest or two was a trivial matter to Him.

The unmatched gallantry of those men who framed our Constitution and our Bill of Rights seems to have been wasted on the men and women in our government today. Their minds of today are definitely not on the things that really matter. Our Senators and Congressmen and Congresswomen have their priorities on satisfying their supporters back home. They can't seem to write a clear bill, they write a piece of legislation and then attach what is called "pork" to it to funnel money to some other pet project in their home state or district.

Honest legislation in Washington D.C. will not happen unless and until the pork barrel is overturned and smashed to smithereens and the lobbyists are run out of town. Everybody knows this but nothing gets done about it, this is another thing that really matters.

Today our governing officials seem ready to use God's name but they are so far removed from righteous governing that there is no comparison and their lack of respect for one another coupled with crude negotiating skills is why Washington remains in gridlock. This is an important thing that really matters!

Jesus Christ warned against this in Luke 6:46 thru 49 NKJ - **46 "But why do you call Me 'Lord, Lord,' and do not do the things which I say? 47 Whoever comes to Me, and hears My sayings and does them, I will show you whom he is like: 48 He is like a man building a house, who dug deep and laid the foundation on the rock. And when the flood arose, the stream beat vehemently against that house, and could not shake it, for it was founded on the rock. 49 But he who heard and did nothing is like a man who built a house on the earth without a foundation, against which the stream beat vehemently; and immediately it fell. And the ruin of that house was great."**

Our country is still standing by the grace of God and because our founders built it on a firm foundation. For the first couple hundred years immigrants and pioneers appreciated being in this country. You can see in the early histories of America how they gave their children names from the Holy Bible, for example: Adam, Peter, Paul, John, Mary, Elizabeth, Martha, and etcetera, the list is long.

CHAPTER THREE

HOW AMERICA FELL FROM GRACE

Eventually though this custom gave way to later generations naming babies after political figures. This was the first blatant indicator of how family loyalty was beginning to drift away from God and society was becoming more and more secular. Today it seems most of the names are made up names, where they came from and what they mean no one knows. All of these are facts that matter greatly!

Our land has seen a lot of bloodshed beginning with the awful horrendous wars with the Native Americans who realized they were being pushed off of their land. The more secular the nation became the more awful evil problems emerged threatening to ruin what could have been a continuing beautiful dream. The result instead was that the country was drawn into wars that killed our young men by thousands and thousands. We had the Indian wars, French and Indian war, the Spanish-American war and the War between the States. Slavery was one evil that should never have happened.

Then we were dragged into WWI and WWII, The Korean War, Vietnam War, and we are at this writing poised to possibly go into an all-out war with Islam, after 14 years in Iraq, while Iran and North Korea are developing nuclear weapons. Today Islamic State in

Syria (ISIS) has come to our land via electronic influence to kill and/or be killed.

History has shown that when nations especially those claiming to be Christian begin depending more and more on the might of their military and less and less on Divine protection more wars develop.

In the Old Testament the kings would consult the prophets and the prophets would consult with God and He would tell them whether or not to go to war. If they didn't listen to what the prophets told them and they went to war anyway, they lost heavily, if that doesn't seem important or we say it doesn't matter ask the mothers of the dead soldiers. However under the guide of our Creator Israel never lost a war that was sanctioned by God.

THE EARLY AMERICAN SETTLERS FOUGHT THE NATIVE AMERICANS

From the year 1622 warring was off and on until 1818. American Cavalry Troops drove the Cherokee nation off their land in North Carolina, Georgia and Virginia to a new location in Oklahoma in the brutal winter of 1838-1839. Nearly 4,000 Indians died on that inhumane forced march. It became known as the "Trail of Tears".

Well so much for our founding premise and concept that all men are created equal. It would be more accurately stated that all men are created evil. Then we must realize that if God doesn't fix evil it will stay that way.

LISTING THE INDIAN WARS

Powhatan-Confederacy	1622-1644
Pequot War	1637
King Philips War	1675-1678
Pueblo Revolt	1680-1692
French and Indian War	1689-1763
Tuscarora War	1711
Yamasee War	1715-1718
Pontiac's Conspiracy	1763
Lord Dunmore's War	1774
Old Northwest Warfare	1790-1794
Battle of Tippecanoe	1811
Creek War	1814
First Seminole War	1816-1818
French and British War	1754-1763
Revolutionary War	1775-1783
War between the States	1861-1865
Spanish - American War	1866-1898
WWI	1914-1918
WWII	1939-1945
Korean War	1950-1953
Vietnam War	1955-1975 *a matter of debate

In light of the scriptures from the Holy Bible we must not forget that it is God who raises up nations and it is God who takes them down. He takes them down for disobedience or after they have fulfilled His purpose for raising them up. The Indians apparently had fulfilled their time of free roaming in this country. Perhaps it was the worshipping of the earth, astrology, mythology, fortune telling, and etcetera that caused our Creator to take their land away from them. We do know that it did happen to the American Indians. Where does that leave us in the United States today? Do some of us worship the earth, astrology, mythology, fortune telling and etcetera? Will God our Creator take this land away from us too? God has commanded us to obey Him in Deuteronomy 12:32.

CHAPTER FOUR
ISRAEL MIGRATING

There is little doubt in the minds of many white Anglo Saxon professing Christians that God gave this land we call the United States of America to us.

Many histories have been written tracking the movement of Ancient Israel from ancient Assyria where they had been taken into exile from Israel in 722 B.C. Ancient Israel migrated 1700 miles up the Danube River and some settled in Scotland, Ireland, Norway, Sweden, Finland, Denmark, Wales, England, Belgium, France and some in Spain and Italy. They became known as the ten "lost tribes" of Israel.

The white English speaking people came to be dominant in most of these countries where the Gaelic language was previously spoken, especially in Scotland, Ireland, Wales, England and France.

This migration of a race of people over a period of approximately 2,000 years coupled with Bible prophecy concerning Israel makes a very strong argument for these nation's whites being descended from Ancient Israel.

Does this mean those who are white skinned are all Jews? Actually that is not true because Jacob whose name was changed to Israel had twelve sons and only one son was named Judah; only his descendants are

Jews. The descendants of the other eleven brothers are not Jews but they are Israelites and they are white skinned. All Israelites are not Jews but all Jews are Israelites. This may account for why our nation and the nation of England helped get the nation of Israel a charter to become an independent Country in 1948.

It doesn't matter that most of the people involved in this charter were aware that they were cousins with the Jews or not because it was God working in their minds and inspiring them toward the same goal. This is the thing that really mattered! God was raising up a new nation by reestablishing Israel after a 2,000 year exile.

When the British General went to Israel to negotiate with the Turks who had occupied the land during the Ottoman Empire, the General found the land deserted, the Turks had left, so the word went out and Jews from all over the world began to come there to pioneer a new Israel. This could not have happened unless God had given them the land of their ancestors. Knowing history is important and it really matters!

Another important thing that really matters is that a nation that obeys God will not have to fight wars. God once referred to Israel as His sheltered ones and He protected them; obedience from the people is what really mattered.

2 Kings 19:30,31,35 NKJ - **30** And the remnant who have escaped of the house of Judah shall again take root downward, and bear fruit upward. **31** For out of Jerusalem shall go a remnant, and those who escape

from Mount Zion. The <u>zeal of the LORD</u> of hosts will do this.' **35** And it came to pass on a certain night that the angel of the LORD went out, and killed in the camp of the Assyrians one hundred and eighty-five thousand; and when *people* arose early in the morning, there were the corpses--all dead.

Even though the founding fathers of our country did a lot of things right, they did not come close to the full package of what Jesus Christ expected of true Christians in the first century Common Era.

The pilgrims from the start may have had good intentions but they missed the mark, they lacked obedience to God. Approximately 150 years before our founding fathers wrote the Declaration of Independence signed on July 4, 1776 they were at war.

The early settlers were at odds with the Native Americans within two years of being here and from about 1622 onward it was almost constant on again - off again war as they fought and bled and died to settle in this land. (The Constitution was not signed until September 17, 1787).

The first Indian war called the Powhatan Confederacy War was fought from 1622 to 1644 in Virginia, the Colonists just barely won.

Then another one was fought in Connecticut and Rhode Island called the Pequot War in 1637. The prisoners of this war were sold as slaves to plantation owners in Bermuda.

The next Indian War was in Massachusetts and Rhode Island and it was called King Philip's War fought from 1675 to 1678.

This next war was fought from 1680 through 1692 between the Mexican Spanish and the Pueblo natives in Arizona and New Mexico. The Mexicans reconquered the territory in 1692.

The war between 1689 and 1763 is known as the French and Indian War fought in the Eastern Woodlands (Appalachia). The war between the French and the British was fought on North American soil to seize the land between 1754 and 1763. The Algonquian Indian tribes allied with the French and the Iroquois Indians sided with the British. The American Indian tribes covering a large portion of North America spoke a common language.

All five wars mentioned above were fought on American soil the first 143 years after the pilgrims landed.

Could these wars have been prevented? The answer is yes, quite possibly! Why do we say that? Because these pilgrimming Israelites had the Holy Bible. The Geneva version was printed first in 1560 then revised and reprinted in 1599. The King James Version was printed first in 1611 and was drafted by the Anglican Church, so we know there were some Bibles on board the Mayflower, the ship they came on when they came to Plymouth Rock in 1620. The complete King James Bible was being printed and distributed for nine years before their departure from England.

William Bradford became the first governor of the New England colonies. Governor Bradford and the Colonists were professing Christians of the Protestant variety, which means they were at variance with the Roman Catholic Church. They were also at variance with some of the Ten Commandments and one very important commandment namely the fourth commandment which was one that really mattered, it could have saved them a lot of grief.

Exodus 31:13 thru 17 NKJ - **13** "Speak also to the children of Israel, saying: 'Surely My Sabbaths you shall keep, for it *is* a sign between Me and you throughout your generations, that *you* may know that I *am* the LORD who sanctifies you. **14** You shall keep the Sabbath, therefore, for *it is* holy to you. Everyone who profanes it shall surely be put to death; for whoever does *any* work on it, that person shall be cut off from among his people. **15** Work shall be done for six days, but the seventh *is* the Sabbath of rest, holy to the LORD. Whoever does *any* work on the Sabbath day, he shall surely be put to death. **16** Therefore the children of Israel shall keep the Sabbath, to observe the Sabbath throughout their generations *as* a perpetual covenant. **17** It *is* a sign between Me and the children of Israel forever; for *in* six days the LORD made the heavens and the earth, and on the seventh day He rested and was refreshed.' "

Even though the colonists had rejected the Pope and the Apostate Catholic Church they still blindly clung to the Catholic imposed day of rest, the day of pagan sun worship. Sunday was never sanctioned by God which is the only way a day can be made holy.

Without a shadow of doubt God would have blessed them beyond their wildest dreams if they had obeyed Him by keeping the Sabbath Day holy. You cannot keep something holy that is not holy to begin with; Sunday is not holy.

CHAPTER FIVE
SABBATH COMES TO NEWPORT

Stephen Mumford was Pastor of the Bell Lane Seventh Day Baptist Church in London. In 1664 he and his wife came to the new land and settled in Rhode Island and began to preach the validity of the true Sabbath to the Colonists.

As each family became convinced of the true Sabbath they began to separate themselves from the Sunday Church and met by themselves on Saturday to worship God. Obeying God is very important to Him and it really matters.

Luke 16:13 NKJ – (Jesus said), **13 No servant can serve two masters; for either he will hate the one and love the other, or else he will be loyal to the one and despise the other. You cannot serve God and mammon."**

God sent Stephen Mumford to the colonies to introduce the true Sabbath to the people who were earnestly seeking Him. The true Sabbath was ordained by God and many of the people began leaving their former association to worship God on the seventh day. For the first time in their lives they were keeping the fourth commandment and receiving blessings for their obedience.

The first official Sabbatarian congregation was founded on American soil at Newport, Rhode Island in 1671.

Stephen Mumford was the human instrument used by God to establish a new protestant denomination in America where it took root, grew and expanded. Here in America the Seventh Day Baptists were free to worship and extol the fourth commandment as is commanded by God in the Holy Bible and was written by the finger of God.

Exodus 20:8 NKJ - 8 "Remember the Sabbath day, to keep it holy.

Deuteronomy 5:12 NKJ - 12 'Observe the Sabbath day, to keep it holy, as the LORD your God commanded you.

Mark 2:27,28 NKJ - 27 And He (Jesus) said to them, **"The Sabbath was made for man, and not man for the Sabbath. 28 Therefore the Son of Man is also Lord of the Sabbath."** (It had been Jesus Christ Himself who took his finger and wrote the Ten Commandments on stone).

As the country spread out westward and southward the Seventh Day Baptist Churches were also raised up along with the others. The parent congregation at Newport, Rhode Island boasted of 40 members in 1692. It was from the Seventh Day Baptist Church that we got the Church of God Seventh Day and the Seventh Day Adventists, plus several smaller seventh day church corporations.

Eventually the Seventh Day Baptists formed a headquarters at Salem, West Virginia and Columbus, Ohio.

WHAT WENT WRONG

William Bradford was the first governor of the colonies in our land and from all indications he was a religious man. One can only imagine what would have transpired if he had become a Sabbath keeper.

What would the early years of our Country have been like if they had treated the Native Americans right and educated them instead of cheating them?

The Indians and the white man could have lived side by side and avoided the awful bloody wars that they had.

If it were possible to take a body count of all the young men our Country has lost in all the wars that we have fought the number of deaths would be horrific. We lost our most valuable resource in losing the young energetic, optimistic men in our country to all these senseless wars in nearly every generation.

We are now dealing with a new generation of young people in a new century, some are already middle aged, and some grew up during the Vietnam War thinking there was no future for them. Some still sleep under bridges at night and some sleep in parking decks or on grates in our cities.

Thousands opted out of trying and became potheads, some became heroin or cocaine addicts, others took LSD and alcohol has played a role in these destructive results. Their minds became mush and their flesh could no longer function properly and we watched as some committed suicide. Thousands of parents have stood over the graves of their teenage children weeping over their loss and the love, the energy and the effort they had expended to guide their youngster to adulthood; it was all futile, just wasted effort. The only comfort to a situation such as this is to search the mind in retrospect for the things in that relationship that were most important and may have really mattered.

The love between a parent and a child is a day to day achievement and it really matters knowing that without a warning a relationship between parent and child, which is a fragile life, can end and all that is left are the memories. There are no guarantees! Thanks be unto God that memories linger, they are personal and if they are the right kind they can be comforting. One of the main things in life that really matters most is that we live every day so as not to have any regrets when at night we close our eyes to sleep.

We say this because we know that we are not promised any tomorrow, <u>all we have is today</u> and at night even today has passed.

Ephesians 4:26,27 ASB - **26** BE ANGRY, AND *yet* DO NOT SIN; do not let the sun go down on your anger, **27** and do not give the devil an opportunity.

After fifty years of being gone from this life most people are not remembered nor do they leave a notable honorable legacy. It is as Solomon has said, man is born and lives but a few days then lays down his life and is forgotten. Ecclesiastes 9:5 NKJ - **5** For the living know that they will die; but the dead know nothing, and they have no more reward, for the memory of them is forgotten.

What really matters is that we leave behind an accomplishment, something that is worthwhile to the betterment of mankind, something that will bear a name for many years to come, something besides a granite stone with a carved inscription with a name, and a date and a few words.

When we are in our senior years and we review our lives we think about the things that have mattered to us and the achievements of other people. What has been achieved will be separated into several categories, one category would be things **that matter**, the second category would be things that **really matter**, and the third category would be things that **really-really matter**.

God does not usually meddle in our business but if we consult with Him everyday things will go a whole lot better. All thoughts, ideas and inspiration come from Him through our thought processes if we are on His wave length.

CHAPTER SIX
REGULATING SOCIETY

We need to have a look at today's politics and philosophy because many of these ideas are tilting our nation toward becoming another socialist country. Socialist countries have elections but they are always rigged and fraudulent. The voters usually have a choice between evil and evil in the candidates. As we look into the fish bowl of candidates running for office we become more and more concerned for ourselves and for our country; this really matters!

Regardless of who gets elected in socialist nations the government is usually always repressive. We have seen examples of how viciously President Obama has attacked some of our freedoms such as freedom to bear arms, freedom to speak, freedom to choose our healthcare, causing employers to cut their employees hours so small that we can't earn enough money to pay the bills.

Obama with his socialist ideas has further crippled the working class and made many of them dependent on government aid for their livelihood and healthcare. The whole idea behind socialism is to take away our freedom, our independence and make us a ward of the state; this is pure and simple socialism and this is how it works. First of all the government will force us into its healthcare system and then take away our guns. Then the government will tell us what to do and when, this also includes worship, where you will live, where you will go to school, etcetera. Anything else we may want to do, whatever it is, forget it, as it may not be allowed! We will work for the government, we will buy our food from the government, we will use the doctors selected by the government and the government will tell us what we can and cannot do.

With socialism life is regulated from the time you get up in the morning until you go to bed at night. The only relief from this cloud of repression hanging over us is when we are sleeping at night because during our waking hours we are constantly aware we are a slave under the control of the government.

Under socialism we are no longer free, our freedoms have disappeared and have been taken away. This is what Barak Obama meant in his campaign speeches before he was elected president of our country. Obama said, he had a plan to fundamentally transform America. Was anyone listening, did anyone catch his words? Did any news reporter ask him what he meant by "transform America"? It seems now thousands regret that they ever voted for him because the hours of their work week have been shortened nearly in half or to a 29 hour work week. Many people can't make their payments on their bills and they can't afford their so called "affordable healthcare" either, nor can they keep their doctor under Obama's plan. If this affordable healthcare act is so wonderful how come Obama and his friends are exempt from this law? Some of us were willing to sign over our lives to this man for many promises and benefits but what a huge price to pay! What a huge disappointment! Satan promises benefits too with a huge price to pay!

We should have the mindset to do as Jesus did with Peter in Matthew 16:23 NKJ - **23** But He (Jesus) turned and said to Peter, **"Get behind Me, Satan! You are an offense to Me, for you are not mindful of the things of God, but the things of men."**

Adolescent minds, like the mind of Obama, being given authority to play games in the real world playing with real people's lives can and have caused a lot of hurt and loss and pain to a lot of people.

Under our system of government we are forced to hold elections and choose people we hope will be qualified to fulfill the duties and obligations of the offices we elect them to, but very often that is not the case. Maybe these people were voted into office because they could speak well and say the right thing, maybe their outward appearance was the best, or maybe they gave us something we didn't have to pay for. The question of course is, "How would God want me to view and vote for a person running for political office"? This is the important question that really matters!

CHAPTER SEVEN
OBAMA'S HISTORY

After Obama studied socialism under Saul Alinsky and learned how to be a street organizer, a metaphor for rabble rouser, he began attending church at Jeremiah Wright's church which was a den of rabble rousers and their mantra was to shout "God damn America".

When Obama started his campaign running for president he threw Jeremiah Wright under the bus so to speak and all the bad publicity ruined Jeremiah's ministry and his credibility as a minister, and he was put out of business in Chicago and he left the state.

To get a clear picture of the muddled mind that Obama has we need to know how it got this way. Obama was a pampered child growing up in Hawaii with nothing to do but dawdle away the hours in the sun.

When Obama became old enough to begin taking an interest in how things work in society he did not have the right mentors.

It is obvious his mind got clouded with the idea that those in charge of our government are also in charge of all the money so he had to find out how to get there.

His hero's became men like Saul Alinsky and the Rev. Jeremiah Wright learning how to bamboozle the public and force them to acquiesce to his demands. Politics was the perfect answer! He thrust himself into it with relish. Politics provided him with the opportunity to throw himself into this fantasy world where he could envision himself rising to the top and really being somebody.

In his early college years he was already studying Islam. Apparently he never became a devout Muslim nor did he become a true Christian.

It became apparent that Obama's goal, his mission, was to study the law of the land in order to thwart it. Apparently he believed if he could ever become an elected official to a political office he could get his own way by perverting the intent of any law he didn't like personally.

Not only that but he became quite artful at lying. In giving any speech he could look you straight in the eye and throw out lie after lie and never break stride, blink or pause for a breath of air as long as he has his teleprompter out front. Hillary Clinton also has this craft down pat by constantly rehearsing what she wants to say.

It is sad in a way but comical too when several months after their speeches are given all of their lies have been exposed. The news people replay their speeches and the lies that were told make them look like fools. They simply have no shame, no conscience and no principles!

Why is it that politicians seem to feel the need to master the craft of lying? It could be because Hitler was an example of a successful liar; his modus-operandi and belief was that if you tell a lie convincingly enough often enough people will begin to believe it to be the truth.

The principle of truth really matters to some but not for all because for some reason many people do not care if they lie or not.

Every time a lie is told Satan the devil is involved, it means someone has come under his influence, which also means they have turned their back on God. That is a condemning, scary situation to put yourself into.

Lying is not only coming from some politicians, or from some ministers but from all sorts of ordinary people. Anyone can lie and have done so in the past but know that lying is a sin and sin is a transgression of the law and death is the penalty which calls for repentance. Romans 6:23 NKJ - **23 For the wages of sin *is* death, but the gift of God *is* eternal life in Christ Jesus our Lord.**

John 8:44 NKJ – (Jesus also said,) **44 You (liars) are of *your* father the devil, and the desires of your father you want to do. He was a murderer from the beginning, and *does not* stand in the truth, because there is no truth in him. When he speaks a lie, he speaks from his own *resources,* for he is a liar and the father of it.**

The largest, most wide spread, most profound swindle on earth is in the merchandising of religion. "Dig deep" the television Evangelists shout at anyone watching the television screen, "sow the seeds" is their metaphor for 'sending money'. Never mind that you may not have enough "seeds" left to plant in your own garden. (A metaphor for feeding and clothing your children). The Evangelists tell you a great, giant blessing will come to you this week or next, just keep the faith, and keep "sowing the seeds", they shout. They are merchandising a parable of the sower. Matthew 13:3 thru 9 NKJ - **3** Then He (Jesus) spoke many things to them in parables, saying: **"Behold, a sower went out to sow. 4 And as he sowed, some** *seed* **fell by the wayside; and the birds came and devoured them. 5 Some fell on stony places, where they did not have much earth; and they immediately sprang up because they had no depth of earth. 6 But when the sun was up they were scorched, and because they had no root they withered away. 7 And some fell among thorns, and the thorns sprang up and choked them. 8 But others fell on good ground and yielded a crop: some a hundredfold, some sixty, some thirty. 9 He who has ears to hear, let him hear!"**

MENTORING WITH THE DEVIL

No one can really understand our president unless one knows about Saul Alinsky. As young impressionable college students Barak Obama and Hillary Rhodam (Clinton) fell under his tutelage and his sway. Then their thinking and values began to change concerning America.

President Obama has followed the Alinsky model as he has drafted his own rules for revolution which he calls "fundamentally transforming America".

So far the President has not been able to transform America but he has caused a lot of hurt and poverty especially in mining areas of the Country and a huge disappointment to too many people. Oil, coal, gasoline and natural gas is not "green energy" so Obama wants to prevent any method of collecting this material from the earth from happening.

Obama began his political career by getting elected to the U.S. Senate from Illinois which put him right where he wanted to be in Washington D.C. where he could observe and plan his next jump on the ladder of politics.

His wife Michelle was quoted by a reporter as saying "Barak is not a politician first and foremost, he is a community activist exploring the viability of politics to make change." Barak was said to have responded, "I take that observation as a compliment". Many questions that need to be asked is how did Barak Obama make it to the top of the ladder so fast? How did he beat Hillary Clinton in becoming the Democratic nominee for president in 2008 when he was virtually unknown? How did a new political newcomer go so far and so fast in such a short period of time without any experience and without any answers? How much lying and cheating with back room dealings went on to make this election go in his direction? Later, when Obama became President voter fraud and IRS intervention became a big issue in his bid for reelection, but they got away with their lies and manipulation of the truth, and their plan for a different government, a socialist transformed government was what they had in mind.

Why is our president so willing to please Vladimir Putin (Russian leader), Iran and the Islamic philosophy? Satan promises benefits but with a huge price to pay! What promises did Satan make to Barak Obama? Has Obama sold his soul to the devil? We have not seen the end of this relationship yet! Mark 8:37 – (Jesus said), **37 Or what will a man give in exchange for his soul?**

After Barak Obama was elected to the presidency he did little else but work on the greatest swindle ever put over on the American public with the aid of his chief Architect Jonathan Gruber for two years. This new healthcare bill was also done in secret as no one read the 11,000 pages of regulations bill before it was voted on by Congress on a Sunday afternoon. Nancy Pelosi, the Speaker of the House said, *"We have to pass the bill so you can find out what is in it ...."* 'USA Today' wrote that if you made the mistake of printing it, it would reach three feet high.

Later Jonathan Gruber publically bragged that it was passed due to the stupidity of the American people and he laughed all the way to the bank for he reportedly received $4 million from the tax payers to oversee the drafting of this document designed to force socialized medicine on a gullible public. The first important step in transforming America is to devise a government healthcare; the Chief Supreme Court Justice, John Roberts knows this to be true.

Now at this writing Obama is turning up the heat trying to take our guns away again! Also the next important step to transforming America is to outlaw all guns. Nearly everyone knows what happened in Europe when they took the guns away, Hitler took them over and began selective mass executions.

Once the government gets completely in charge of everyone's healthcare and they take away our guns it does not matter whether you call it revolution or transformation it is socialism or communism.

It does not matter what the radical left call themselves all of it means they want to take our freedom away. Call it Communism, Socialism, new left, liberal, social justice activists, or progressives; all of it is the work of the devil and Saul Alinsky was his prophet and Barak Obama and Hillary Clinton were Saul Alinsky's students.

The leftist agenda is not new but it is radical. They believe in the radical illusion that they, through political power can create a new world, just blend the races and you will have harmony and peace, then they, the elected, can rule as god in their manufactured utopia. Is this the reason Obama will not close our southern border?

In the Holy Bible in the book of Genesis Adam and Eve were first to be lied to with this idea of being like God. Genesis 3:5 NKJ - 5 For God knows that in the day you eat of it your eyes will be opened, and you will be like God, knowing good and evil.

Up to this time God was showing them everything that was harmful to them and instructing them to avoid such things. But Satan told them they would be like gods and could know 'good from evil' on their own without God's help.

We all know it did not work for them it has not worked since and it will not work now. Anyone who thinks taking advice from Satan is a good idea is a fool.

Alinsky taught his students, Barak and Hillary that life is a corrupting process and that those who fear corruption fear life. He espoused that since life is corrupt, everyone is corrupt and corruption is just business as usual, another huge lie!

Vladimir Lenin who massacred 20 million of his fellow countrymen to bring Communism to Russia was a great hero to Saul Alinsky.

Fidel Castro was another of his heroes. He loved to recite a favorite slogan from Mao Zedong of China which was, "Political power grows out of the barrel of a gun".

Obama was schooled under the slogan of Lenin who came to power shouting "one man, one vote, one time" the exact same credo of Adolf Hitler who after he was elected shut down the voting booths forever.

We are not lost on what Hitler did, he justified every means he thought necessary to achieve his goals. He ordered mass executions, built concentration camps and ordered the literal liquidation of entire social classes, some estimates number the slain at 15 million, half of them were Jews.

Alinsky schooled his students, two of which were Barak and Hillary not to try selling socialism by the title or people would know what they were up to. They were instructed to call it "progressivism", "economic democracy" and "social justice" and to work within the system until you can accumulate enough power to destroy it.

Most of the leftist liberal leaders in our government today would replace our government with a democracy of their own creation like Lenin did, and Mao Zedong, and Adolf Hitler and Fidel Castro. What is the reason Barak Obama has made peace with the Castro brothers and does it really matter?

Alinsky advised his students, "You are at war with the system, don't confront it, join it and undermine it from within by preaching a necessity of change itself". First it's a must to make a change in the healthcare system, regulate the medical services, and then regulate the food supply. The next step is getting the guns out of the possession of the people leaving them helpless. Does this sound like the mindset of Barak Obama? Revolutionary war must be conducted through deception. Obama and Hillary seem to believe the better you can lie, the more virtuous you are.

Honest people who attempt to break into politics are at a great disadvantage, they believe America is about tolerance and compromise and bringing working partnerships together, they are not at war with the system yet, they have seen that it does need improvements using a lot of thought, a lot of prayer, and to ask God for wisdom. Asking God for the right kind of cooperation our system can and would work beautifully!

When people are at war there is no middle ground as they are in a mental state called "frenzy", they perceive the opponents to their cause as real enemies on a battlefield; and realize that they must discredit and destroy them so they set about demonizing them.

Demonizing and discrediting is the weapon of choice for leftists as they set out to destroy any new gullible politician desiring to be a public servant. Their goal is not to let any new upstart politician of a different opinion succeed.

If a man or a woman has the mind-set for justice and believe in fairness and inclusion stay out of politics! They will twist and spin everything you say until they have shot your credibility and your reputation will be in shreds; they can destroy your faith in America. They like to use another of Lenin's sayings, "The Capitalists will sell us the rope to hang them with".

In American politics we have one side at war with the system while the other is trying to enforce the rules of fairness and pluralism. It is nothing more than Satan trying to tear America down; we must resist. We need to resist! But how and what to resist means we must be informed and stay alert. Simply put "good versus evil". The twisted demonic radical left have deceived themselves into believing they can create their own utopia, or "heaven on earth". It must be emphasized that every day they sell this lie to a gullible public.

For a society to prosper it needs people like: Henry Ford, Thomas Edison, Bill Gates and Steve Jobs. Men like these men are what Alinsky called "the haves" while he referred to the labor force and unemployed as "the have nots". Alinsky hated the "haves" because he saw them as oppressors of the "have nots", sitting on the top of their hierarches as the upper class in both race and gender. He apparently borrowed some of this thinking from Karl Marx. Marx wanted the middle class, which owned the factories and provided the jobs, to be taken over by the ruling class which is of course the government and that is what happened in Eastern Europe and Russia.

When this happens we have only two classes of people; the ruling class and the slave class. The government keeps all the profits until eventually all the equipment wears out and breaks down and many jobs disappear then the country sinks into depressed poverty; after that we have a nation in ruin.

Capitalism has proven it is the only system of governing that works! Satan has destroyed many governments before America and he wants to destroy America too. Many representatives in Washington are not supporting the people for the good of the people, they are minions of Satan. Some of the most prominent obstructionists are from New York, Nevada, California and other states too.

One main evil to a peaceful functioning society is contention, squabbling back and forth among the political parties as this keeps them from compromising and arriving at wise decisions. Understanding what is happening to our land is important and it really matters.

Karl Marx, the father of Communism, in his diseased mind, viewed all past history as a history of class struggles, the oppressor and the oppressed existing in steadfast opposition to one another which has caused massive death, ruin and loss throughout the world. It is dangerous as we have seen what Karl Marx's philosophy has caused in Russia and Eastern Europe in the 20th century. This line of thinking has proven to be the foundation of all radical belief and its destructive agendas. The Communist agenda leads to the idea that all governments are evil and should be overthrown, apparently they don't see themselves as being evil. This idea is why constant revolutions take place around the earth as peace is interrupted everywhere; which is exactly what Satan wants.

Jesus gave us warning about tribulation in Matthew 24:6 NKJ - **6 And you will hear of wars and rumors**

of wars. See that you are not troubled; for all *these things* must come to pass, but the end is not yet.

As we have seen ever since the U.S.A has been established our country has lost a lot of our young men in nearly every generation because of fighting off some enemy so we could keep our country safe and free. <u>Remembering important things like this really does matter</u>!

Something else that matters is that one more epitaph that Alinsky taught Barak and Hillary which is "Power is to be seized." Alinsky preached with great stress to his students, "The present world will not allow justice to be realized, sooner or later immoral, illegal, even violent means are required to achieve the radical goal".

Now we begin to see why blacks, Muslims and haters of righteousness escape prosecution so often under the Obama Administration and why so many executive orders of a quirky nature have been written by this President.

Obama apparently feels justified in being judge, jury, and prosecutor, but "liberator" would be a better word as criminals, Taliban and Al-Qaeda prisoners go free as some are able to stay in the U.S. to resume terror or go back home and resume terror.

Looking back, into our history, can a time be remembered when other Presidents had two black secretaries of state, three female secretaries of state, a black male and a black female as the nation's top law enforcement officer and six Muslim aids working in the White House?

It is a false narrative to describe our American society in terms of the "have's" and the "have nots" and to imply that there are immovable barriers that prevent "have nots" from bettering themselves financially and socially. There is no justification for Alinsky's radical war on society! It must have been piped into his head by the devil.

David Horowitz said it best when he wrote that in American democracy social and economic divisions are between the "Can" and the "Can nots", the "Do's" and the "Do nots", the "Wills" and the "Will nots".

David categorized it this way because the vast majority of today's wealthy Americans are the first affluent generation in their families and they have created their own wealth. They did not come from wealthy families and did not inherit what they own.

While on television President Obama suggested "The government did everything for them". To describe wealthy Americans as wealth earners and wealth creators is to describe them accurately. There is no need for radical upheaval and social change in America as opportunity and hard work is the answer. It is not wise by any particular standard to flood the White House or any government office, local, state, or federal with people of one race, or one color or one religion because not many of one race or creed have been previously qualified to hold such an important position; nor can they adequately represent all American citizens.

Today our Senate and House of Representatives are loaded with "can nots" and "do nots" and "will nots" so much so that nothing can be done, nothing does get done and nothing will get done!

The next five years will probably serve as a barometer to show either a revival of good sense and dedication to our country from Washington D.C. or those of us who are still standing could hear the tolling of the final bell as this once proud and powerful country slips on downward into hell like a sinking ship.

When selecting someone for an elective office or appointment to an important office, it really matters that they have stellar character, experience in a related field, and a dedication and love for the Country.

Barack Obama had none of these qualifications and neither did most of the people he appointed to office. If his idea was to prove to the world that people of his race and his religion could run this Country he certainly proved the exact opposite.

Obama's theme coming into office was "hope and change", "redistribution" and "fundamentally transforming America". His plan was never to make America better it was to abscond as much as possible from the "have's" through "executive order" and give it to the "have nots" and to the middle Eastern Muslims.

Obama's plan is to drive the Country into as much debt as possible during his term and to hood-wink the gullible public into a government health care scheme and if possible take away the guns. The worst of his schemes were to weaken our military to the level it was prior to WWII.

His legacy to transform America takes the shape of trying to weaken the Country, break it down and make it vulnerable to Islamic terrorists and foreign invasion and get out of town as soon as his term is over.

There is little doubt among those watching these revolting developments that Obama wants Hillary to replace him when his term in office is over because she has been trained by Alinsky on how to finish the job. Obama has done his part now it will be up to Hillary to finish rolling the country over into a Socialist state.

America's first black President will go down in infamy on the pages of history as a community organizer, a life-long associate of political radicals, who ran a successful campaign on a platform of changing America's status quo, not defending the country or trying to improve it, but to change it his way.

Apparently Alinsky learned a lot from Lenin for his mission was a mission of destruction too, Lenin's idea was to not refute your opponent "But wipe him from the face of the earth".

Those who have a demonic philosophy such as this, if they were smart at all would realize that this game can be played from both ends and often has been. Many of us have been witness to the fact that what goes around comes around. Matthew 26:52 NKJ - **52** But Jesus said to him, **"Put your sword in its place, for all who take the sword will perish by the sword"**.

Another thing of bleak stupidity is how radicals like Obama and Hillary think they can create a paradise of perfect justice and harmony, when they and all their cohorts would know they used unscrupulous, deceiving, conniving and ruthless means to get there. It would be a house of cards to use a metaphor!

Utopia, a garden of Eden, paradise on earth is a fantasy in the minds of emotionally unbalanced radical people who somehow believe they could provide food to every hungry soul on earth and shelter and clothe them. They could end bigotry and all human conflict so in their feeble troubled minds every possible sacrifice to climb to the top in government is worth it. They actually believe that if they can only make it to the top they can become King or Queen of their Utopia.

Lenin, Stalin, Hitler, Mussolini and others were infected with this satanic delusion, that it is okay and necessary to break rules of normalcy to accomplish the goal of building a utopia and overthrow the existing order of countries. The end justifies the means just as Alinsky taught his students "radicals are in a permanent war and in war the end justifies almost any means". This means utopia for them and slavery for the people!

Alinsky believed that once a student is convinced to break the law they are on their way to becoming revolutionaries and they will do what their leader wants.

He was one who should know, he took his basic training from Frank Nitti, Al Capone's "enforcer". The activities of the mob were always directed at the rich which in their minds made it necessary and okay.

The more honorable and more noble these men appeared to be the easier it was to justify mass murder and carnage of every sort. A true committed radical therefore is automatically an outlaw and doesn't care about anyone else that is not involved with their agenda.

Alinsky's young revolutionaries were told not to worry about the legality or morality of their actions only the practical effects of their actions. They believe the evil they do is already justified by the fact that they do it for the "salvation of mankind".

The ideas they are given by professors like Alinsky are seductive enough to persuade some of them that it's alright to lie, to commit fraud, mayhem and murder in order to enter their envisioned utopian promised land. What a huge incentive to commit evil! It is doubtful if there exists on this earth any higher delusionary arrogance than this, it is a mind totally given over to Satan.

For proof it is written in scripture Ezekiel chapter 28 NKJ - **1** The word of the LORD came to me again, saying, **2** "Son of man, say to the prince of Tyre, 'Thus says the LORD GOD: "Because your heart *is* lifted up, and you say, 'I *am* a god, I sit *in* the seat of gods, in the midst of the seas,' Yet you *are* a man, and not a god, though you set your heart as the heart of a god **3** (Behold, you *are* wiser than Daniel! There is no secret that can be hidden from you! **4** With your wisdom and your understanding you have gained riches for yourself, and gathered gold and silver into your treasuries; **5** by your great wisdom in trade you have increased your riches, and your heart is lifted up because of your riches)," **6** 'Therefore thus says the LORD GOD: "Because you have set your heart as the heart of a god, **7** behold, therefore, I will bring strangers against you, the most terrible of the nations; and they shall draw their swords against the beauty of your wisdom, and defile your splendor. **8** They shall throw you down into the Pit, and you shall die the death of the slain in the midst of the seas. **9** "Will you still say before him who slays you, 'I *am* a god'? But you *shall be* a man, and not a god, in the hand of him who slays you. **10** You shall die the death of the uncircumcised by the hand of aliens; for I have spoken," says the LORD GOD.' " **11** Moreover the word of the LORD came to me, saying, **12** "Son of man, take up a lamentation for the king of Tyre, and say to him, 'Thus says the LORD GOD: "You *were* the seal of perfection, full of wisdom and perfect in beauty. **13** You were in Eden, the garden of God; every precious stone *was* your covering: The sardius, topaz, and diamond, beryl, onyx, and jasper, sapphire, turquoise, and emerald with gold. The workmanship of your timbrels and pipes was prepared for you on the day you were created. **14** "You *were* the anointed cherub who covers; I established you; you were on the holy mountain of GOD; you walked back and forth in the midst of fiery stones. **15** You *were* perfect in your ways from the day you were created, till iniquity was found in you. **16** "By the abundance of your trading you became filled with violence within, and you sinned; therefore I cast you as a profane thing out of the mountain of GOD; and I destroyed you, O covering cherub, from the midst of the fiery stones. **17** "Your heart was lifted up because of your beauty; you corrupted your wisdom for the sake of your splendor; I cast you to the ground, I laid you before kings, that they might gaze at you. **18** "You defiled your sanctuaries by the multitude of your iniquities, by the iniquity of your trading; therefore I brought fire from your midst; it devoured you, and I turned you to ashes upon the earth in the sight of all who saw you. **19** All who knew you among the peoples are astonished at you; you have become a horror, and *shall be* no more forever." ' " **20** Then the word of the LORD came to me, saying, **21** "Son of man, set your face toward Sidon, and prophesy against her, **22** and say, 'Thus says the LORD GOD: "Behold, I *am* against you, O Sidon; I will be glorified in your midst; and they shall know that I *am* the LORD, when I execute judgments in her and am hallowed in her. **23** For I will send pestilence upon her, and blood in her streets; the wounded shall be judged in her midst by the sword against her on every side; then they shall know that I *am* the LORD. **24** "And there shall no longer be a pricking brier or a painful thorn for the house of Israel from among all *who are* around them, who despise them. Then they shall know that I *am* the LORD GOD." **25** 'Thus says the LORD GOD: "When I have gathered the house of Israel from the peoples among whom they are scattered, and am hallowed in them in the sight of the Gentiles, then they will dwell in their own land which I gave to My servant Jacob. **26** And they will dwell safely there, build houses, and plant vineyards; yes, they will dwell securely, when I execute judgments on all those around them who despise them. Then they shall know that I *am* the LORD their GOD." ' "

God is not mocked and world rulers come and go. Several men have tried to conquer and subjugate the world but their remains went back to the elements long ago and they were never crowned king of the earth. Galatians 6:7 NKJ - **7** Do not be deceived, God is not mocked; for whatever a man sows, that he will also reap.

Read the account of how Lucifer rose up and flaunted himself in heaven but he and his minions were banished to the earth and it became their penal colony.

Isaiah chapter 14:12 thru 20 NKJ - **12** "How you are fallen from heaven, O Lucifer, son of the morning! *How* you are cut down to the ground, you who weakened the nations! **13** For you have said in your heart: 'I will ascend into heaven, I will exalt my throne above the stars of God; I will also sit on the mount of the congregation on the farthest sides of the north; **14** I will ascend above the heights of the clouds, I will be like the Most High.' **15** Yet you shall be brought down to Sheol, to the lowest depths of the pit. **16** "Those who see you will gaze at you, *and* consider you, *saying:* '*Is* this the man who made the earth tremble, who shook kingdoms, **17** who made the world as a wilderness and destroyed its cities, *who* did not open the house of his prisoners?' **18** "All the kings of the nations, all of them, sleep in glory, everyone in his own house; **19** but you are cast out of your grave like an abominable branch, *like* the garment of those who are slain, thrust through with a sword, who go down to the stones of the pit, like a corpse trodden underfoot. **20** You will not be joined with them in burial, because you have destroyed your land *and* slain your people. The brood of evildoers shall never be named. (Lucifer became Satan the adversary to God and all God is accomplishing through human beings.)

In our times of meditation, contemplating and understanding over important things that really matter, what can be more important than what really matters to God?

Jeremiah 9:24 NKJ - **24** But let him who glories glory in this, that he understands and knows Me, that I *am* the LORD, exercising lovingkindness, judgment, and righteousness in the earth. For in these I delight," says the LORD.

Some geologists now tell us that the condition of the earth mentioned in Genesis was the first occurrence of a worldwide flood. Genesis 1:2 NKJ - **2** The earth was without form, and void; and darkness *was* on the face of the deep. And the Spirit of God was hovering over the face of the waters.

Some archeologists believe that after Satan and his demons were exiled on the earth they tried to destroy the planet. They killed the dinosaurs and all the huge creatures and wreaked such chaos on earth that God flooded the entire earth to clean it up and buried all the dead creatures. Since spirit beings can't drown and they do not need air to sustain their lives they were marooned on a bleak water covered planet for many-many years until it was time to dry the planet up and create mankind. Earth became a type of penal colony.

Since Satan and his demons have been exiled to the earth Satan has been the ruler of the world and his modus operandi is to <u>destroy everything</u> on the earth. In Noah's day only Noah and his family escaped the second flood along with the animals, birds, etcetera, that were on the ark with them. The Lord God tells us in His Word that there will not be a third flood! The next time evil rises to that level, evil and the implementer of it will be destroyed as it is written in Ezekiel 28.

God created Adam and Eve on this penal colony where there was nothing but evil beings and creatures that could easily kill them. For their protection God designed Adam and Eve a garden to live in that was a utopian spot on the earth where the climate was perfect and food was abundant. They had it all, nuts, berries, peaches, pears, apples, pomegranates, grapes, edible roots and more. They in return maintained the grounds, picked up twigs, etcetera, which was light maintenance. Years later after they came under Satan's influence and had eaten the forbidden fruit they were banished from their beautiful utopian home.

They struggled against the elements for their survival, and as their family grew in numbers life became more difficult. Satan became an influence on Cain, their first born son, causing him to kill his younger brother. With each passing generation life got worse, life became harder and more problematic; it became so bad with wickedness God caused a flood. After about 1400 years we come to a time when God was taking stock of how well His human creation was doing and the situation is described in Genesis 6:5 NKJ - **5** Then the LORD saw that the wickedness of man *was* great in the earth, and *that* every intent of the thoughts of his heart *was* only evil continually.

The account of Noah and the Ark was the second time the entire earth was under water. Genesis 7:11,12 NKJ - **11** In the six hundredth year of Noah's life, in the second month, the seventeenth day of the month, on that day all the fountains of the great deep were broken up, and the windows of heaven were opened. **12** And the rain was on the earth forty days and forty nights. (Proving God had a calendar back then).

After the rain, it took one year plus eleven days (371 days) for the earth to dry up enough so Noah and his family could come out of the Ark. Genesis 8:14 thru 22 NKJ - **14** And in the second month, on the twenty-seventh day of the month, the earth was dried.

15 Then God spoke to Noah, saying, **16** "Go out of the ark, you and your wife, and your sons and your sons' wives with you. **17** Bring out with you every living thing of all flesh that *is* with you: birds and cattle and every creeping thing that creeps on the earth, so that they may abound on the earth, and be fruitful and multiply on the earth." **18** So Noah went out, and his sons and his wife and his sons' wives with him. **19** Every animal, every creeping thing, every bird, *and* whatever creeps on the earth, according to their families, went out of the ark. **20** Then Noah built an altar to the LORD, and took of every clean animal and of every clean bird, and offered burnt offerings on the altar. **21** And the LORD smelled a soothing aroma. Then the LORD said in His heart, "I will never again curse the ground for man's sake, although the imagination of man's heart *is* evil from his youth; nor will I again destroy every living thing as I have done. **22** "While the earth remains, seedtime and harvest, cold and heat, winter and summer, and day and night shall not cease."

Genesis 9:13 thru 17 NKJ - **13** I set My rainbow in the cloud, and it shall be for the sign of the covenant between Me and the earth. **14** It shall be, when I bring a cloud over the earth, that the rainbow shall be seen in the cloud; **15** and I will remember My covenant which *is* between Me and you and every living creature of all flesh; the waters shall never again become a flood to destroy all flesh. **16** The rainbow shall be in the cloud, and I will look on it to remember the everlasting covenant between God and every living creature of all flesh that *is* on the earth." **17** And God said to Noah, "This *is* the sign of the covenant which I have established between Me and all flesh that *is* on the earth."

The rainbow is an important sign and it really matters to God! When a rainbow appears in the sky during or after a rainfall, folks run to see its beauty. Now you know why the rainbow appears, it is a reminder of the eventual end of Satan and evil.

Another thing that really matters to God is His creation. Look at His creation all the way through from top to bottom and notice how every species compliments other species, one thing depends upon another from algae to elephants or ants to fish and fish to birds or visa-versa. In many cases one species depends upon the other for survival whether on land or in the ocean.

ON THE EDGE...Today we live in an age where industry has ruined and polluted many waterways, fossil fuels have polluted our air, our crops are grown on chemical fertilizer and sprayed with insecticides, and all of the residue from these chemicals wash into our creeks and rivers and poison many species of wild life. We eat ducks, geese, and fish, all of which are contaminated by these practices and wonder why many people come down with cancer and other chronic diseases. Our world has been poisoned; the soil is filled with chemicals, the water is polluted and the air we breathe is contaminated. What is worse is that the hearts, minds, and the consciences of the people are drifting farther away from God. <u>All of these things really matter</u>!

CHAPTER EIGHT
AMERICAN ENGLISH

People change! Whether it is within communities, counties, states, or nations the preferences, ideologies, even languages and sometimes religions tend to evolve. This is most evident in languages and ideologies, sometimes due to political pressures.

One chief example of a language evolving is to read the Holy Bible starting with the first edition of the Geneva Bible (1560), then the second edition of the Geneva Bible (1599), then the King James Bible (1611), the English Revised Bible (1885), the New King James Bible (1883), the Amplified Bible and the NIV, plus there are several others in the English language.

In the 5th century a dialect of the Frisian Islands and West Germany was brought into England by the Anglo-Saxon settlers.

Due to all the British colonies around the world the ever always evolving English language is now the official language in 60 sovereign states and provinces. Today it has become the third most common native language of the world behind only Mandarin (standard Chinese), and Spanish. It is the language of the white Anglo Saxon people of the world, it is also spoken by several African and Hispanic countries as a second language.

Many people ask about the Saxons and what was their origin and where did they spring from? We find the answer hidden in plain view in the pages of the Holy Bible.

In the book of Genesis chapter 16 is the account of Abram being persuaded into a consented act of adultery and begetting a child out of wedlock with Hagar his Egyptian maid. Chapter 16:15 and 16 NKJ tell of the birth of Ishmael, **15** So Hagar bore Abram a son; and Abram named his son, whom Hagar bore, Ishmael. **16** Abram *was* eighty-six years old when Hagar bore Ishmael to Abram. God rejected Ishmael to be Abrams descendant. Ishmael means God will hear!

In Genesis chapter 17:15,16,17,19,21 NKJ – **15** Then God said to Abraham, "As for Sarai your wife, you shall not call her name Sarai, but Sarah (Princess) *shall be* her name. **16** And I will bless her and also give you a son by her; then I will bless her, and she shall be *a mother of* nations; kings of peoples shall be from her." **17** Then Abraham fell on his face and laughed, and said in his heart, "Shall *a child* be born to a man who is one hundred years old? And shall Sarah, who is ninety years old, bear *a child?*" **19** Then God said: "No, Sarah your wife shall bear you a son, and you shall call his name Isaac (laughter); I will establish My covenant with him for an everlasting covenant, *and* with his descendants after him. **21** But My covenant I will establish with Isaac, whom Sarah shall bear to you at this set time next year." God said He would establish an everlasting covenant with Isaac.

We pick up this very important biblical story again in Genesis chapter 21:12 NKJ - **12** But God said to Abraham, "Do not let it be displeasing in your sight because of the lad or because of your bondwoman. Whatever Sarah has said to you, listen to her voice; for in Isaac your seed shall be called. (God sent Hagar and Ishmael away).

A further reference is given by the Apostle Paul in Romans 9:6,7 NKJ - **6** But it is not that the word of God has taken no effect. For they *are* not all Israel who *are* of Israel, **7** nor *are they* all children because they are the seed of Abraham; but, *"In Isaac your seed shall be called."*

The prophet Amos had spouted a warning also that the house of Israel was the house of Isaac. Amos 7:16 NKJ - **16** Now therefore, hear the word of the LORD: You say, 'Do not prophesy against Israel, and do not spout against the house of Isaac.' We find another reference to Isaac's status in Hebrews 11:17,18 NKJ - **17** By faith Abraham, when he was tested, offered up Isaac, and he who had received the promises offered up his only begotten *son,* **18** of whom it was said, *"In Isaac your seed shall be called."* The house of Isaac are the descendants of Isaac; the Saxons were the sons of Isaac, Isaac's sons. (Overtime, the "I" was dropped from Isaac and his sons became known as Saac's sons or Saxons.)

These men were not the same as the Old High German SAHS meaning "sword" or "knife". The Teutonic tribes that migrated from ancient Assyria were tall blonde fierce "war men". The word German into English developed from "war man".

Isaac's two sons were Jacob and Esau. Modern Turkey today are the descendants of Esau primarily while Isaac's sons, through Jacob, "Saxons" are dispersed around the earth. (Information according to Dr. W. Holt Yates of Yale University).

The amusing and interesting thing about all of the English speaking sons of Isaac is the differences in their colloquial dialects. A well-traveled salesman can usually tell what state or at least what quadrant of the U.S. a person is from by engaging them in conversation; speaking between countries is also unique such as England, Australia, New Zealand, South Africa, Canada and others.

North America is a big country and from the border with Mexico to the northern tip of Alaska and from the Pacific Coast to the Atlantic Coast there are many, many colloquial phrases and expressions including in Canada.

Crossing into the Canadian border someone speaks by ending a sentence with "heh" or "hey". The implication being "did you understand?"

One example is how people speak to each other in a group or singularly. In Florida where multiple thousands of retirees live as they are in large part from the northern states they usually say "you" in a singular or plural way.

In Georgia you will hear people say "y'all". In Tennessee it evolves into a mixture of "y'all or you all". In Virginia it gives way to only "you all". In the mountains of West Virginia it is just plain old "you" in both singular and plural. In Ohio you will hear "you guys". In Pennsylvania you will hear "youse guys" which gives way to a simple "youse" in New Jersey and so on up the coast into New York and in New England folks say "earl" for oil, that thick syrupy stuff you pour into the crankcase of your "cah" for car. Then again in the southwestern part of the United States they end a sentence with "savvy"? In Australia everyone is a "mate".

So much for truck driver trivia but it does illustrate the various uses of the language of Isaac's sons. This is true in North America and no doubt a similar situation in other parts of the world where Isaac's sons are the dominant people.

The English language is the native tongue of 60 or more countries proving that the so-called "10 lost tribes of Israel" are not lost, we know where they are, we just don't know who they all are. These people who have migrated up the Danube River and spilled over into Europe, the Netherlands, Scotland, Ireland, Wales, Belgium, Norway, Switzerland, Finland, Denmark, England, France etcetera are the co-called lost tribes of Israel. The tragedy of this knowledge is that many people do not know the facts, however they do know where the Jews are, but they are a mixture of Judah, Benjamin and Levi.

The English language is so complex that it just keeps on changing and probably will never stop. Every English speaking Country has words and phrases that are unique to them but they are still English. Not only that but because of the new things that are constantly being invented we have new words, new ways which produce new nouns and new verbs.

It is written that knowledge will be increased in the end times, Daniel 12:4 NKJ - 4 "But you, Daniel, shut up the words, and seal the book until the time of the end; many shall run to and fro, and knowledge shall increase." As we look around knowledge is coming at us with lightning speed from every direction, it is so fast we cannot keep up with it all; for example: Computers, Cell phones, Texting, Facebook and Twitter, Television, Radio with more to come.

It took centuries for all of the facts to get sorted out and find out where the ten tribes disappeared to after Babylon came over and attacked Assyria in 612 B.C. Steven Collins researched this several years ago and wrote an excellent book called "The Lost Ten Tribes of Israel Found".

In ancient Hebrew the word "Isaac" meant laughter and wherever we are on the earth and we are in a country of Isaac's sons you will notice them laughing and joking and having a good time with each other.

Isaac's sons are also fierce competitors in sports and car racing for example; they love to have a relaxing good time as we can tell by the way they throng the stadiums at ball games. They are indeed a happy laughing people.

Laughing was a mark put on them because of Abraham and how he reacted when he was 100 years of age when God announced to him that he and Sarah were going to have a son with Sarah being 90 years of age. This miracle child being the first child of these two people, at their age, was a blessing and a miracle from God that only God could accomplish.

In Genesis 17:5,15 NKJ - **5** No longer shall your name be called Abram, but your name shall be Abraham; for I have made you a <u>father of many nations</u>. **15** Then God said to Abraham, "As for Sarai your wife, you shall not call her name Sarai, but Sarah *shall be* her name. (Sarai became Sarah which means "princess". Abram meant "exalted father" but Abraham meant "father of a multitude".) Both of their names were changed and they were given the covenant of circumcision setting the stage for growing a new race of people to become known as the circumcision, Israel.

God had ordained Abraham as the Father of this race and ordained Sarah as a princess so she now had royal blood in her veins.

Through Isaac, their offspring this race would be identified as "the circumcised or the circumcision". Their grandson, Joseph, became the second highest ruler in Egypt later on and the scepter was given to his brother Judah to rule in the nation of Israel when the nation became established. The nation of Israel was called the circumcision.

CHAPTER NINE
THE ROYAL LINE AND THE PRIESTHOOD

Israel's first king was Saul, a Benjamite, Israel's second king was David, a Jew; every king after David was from the tribe of Judah. This royal line was passed to Judah and today the royal scepter resides in England. Queen Elizabeth is a direct descendant of King David and her husband, Prince Philip is also from the tribe of Judah. They do not practice the Jewish religion even though they both carry the Judah royal blood in their veins. See chart on page 69.

Genesis 49:10 NKJ - **10** The scepter shall not depart from Judah, nor a lawgiver from between his feet, until Shiloh (Christ) comes; and to Him *shall be* the obedience of the people.

IMPORTANT THINGS THAT REALLY MATTER

The Royal Lines from Zarah and Pharez Judah

Judah

Levi
Aaron
(High Priesthood)

The Royal House of ZARAH-JUDAH (The Scarlet Cord) GEN. 38.28

The Royal House of PHAREZ-JUDAH

David

CRETAN KINGS

Solomon — Nathan

TROJAN KINGS* — MILESIAN KINGS

Zedekiah (The King's Daughter) (JER. 43. v. 6)

Simon the Just

FRANKISH KINGS — SCANDINAVIAN KINGS

Joseph (Putative only) — The Virgin Mary

Joseph of Arimathea

Anna

HOUSE OF SKIOLD — HOUSE OF WECTA

KINGS OF IRELAND

Jesus Christ
High Priest
King of Kings
Lord of Lords
"The Lion of the Tribe of Judah"

KINGS OF SCOTLAND

Royal House of TUDOR (or from TROJAN KINGS)

Albert x Victoria, 1840

KINGS OF DENMARK

ROYAL HOUSE OF WINDSOR

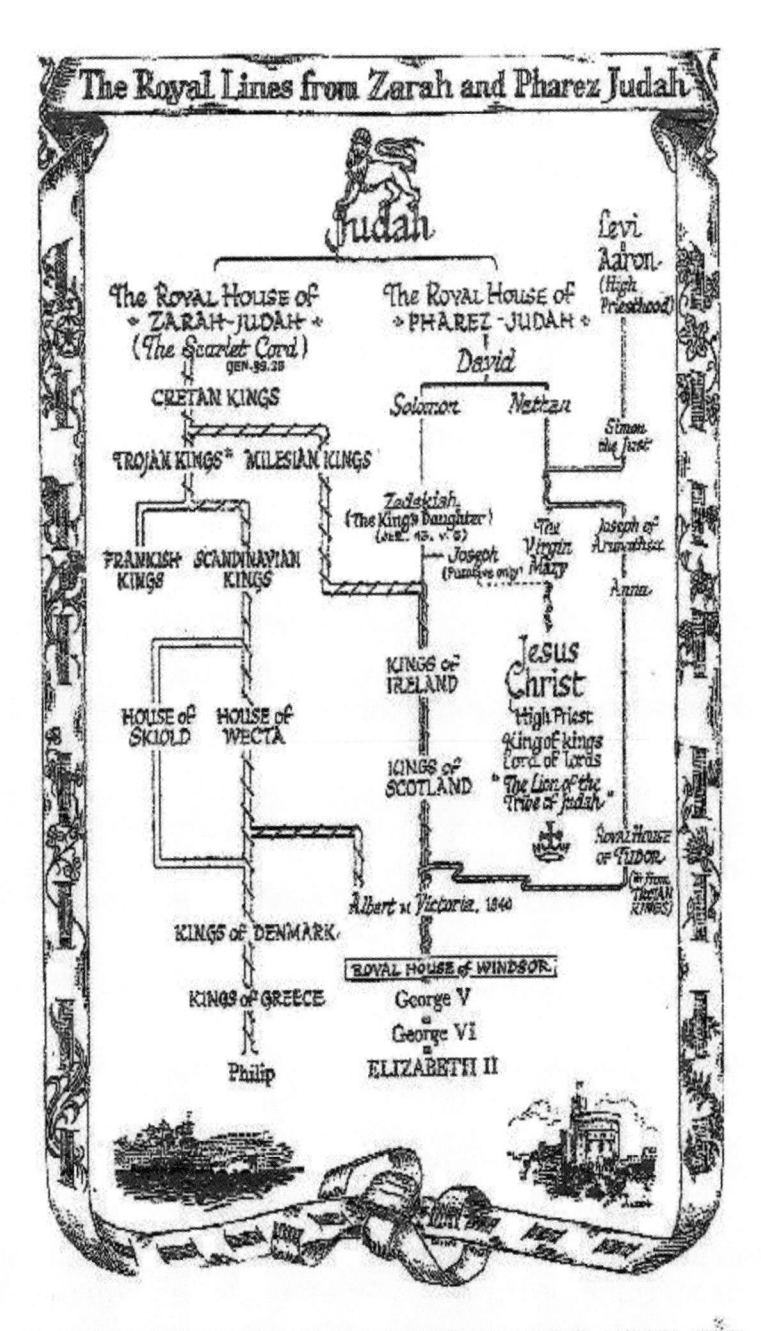

KINGS OF GREECE

George V
=
George VI
=
ELIZABETH II

Philip

*The Royal House of Britain an enduring Dynasty, written by Rev. W. M. H. Milner M.A. – Fifteenth Edition "The Covenant Publishing Co. LTD. 8 Blades Court, Deodar Road, Putney, London SW15 2NU"

CHAPTER TEN

THE GENEALOGY OF JESUS

The genealogy of Jesus Christ through His mother Mary written in Luke 3:23 NKJ - **23** Now Jesus Himself began *His ministry at* about thirty years of age, being (as was supposed) *the* son of Joseph, *the son* of Heli. Luke 3:31 NKJ - **31** *the son* of Melea, *the son* of Menan, *the* <u>son of Mattathah</u>, *the son* of Nathan, *the* <u>son of David</u>.

Luke 3:23,31 should have been translated this way, now Jesus Himself began His ministry at about thirty years of age, being the step son of Joseph, Heli (Mary's father) being a son of Mattathah, and Jesus became a grandson of Heli.

The facts are that Heli was the father of Jesus' mother Mary and the father-in-law of Joseph. Heli was from the lineage of King David carrying both the royal kingly blood line and the priestly blood line in his veins.

This is important information because Jesus was given royal blood and priestly blood through His mother Mary as He had no human father. His conception was a miraculous event performed by the God the Father.

Elizabeth was the mother of John the Baptist and Elizabeth's husband was Zacharias a priest, a descendant of Aaron. Priestly duties could only be performed by a Levite at the temple and the priests could only marry Levite women. Aaron was commissioned by God to be the first priest as Israel was coming out of Egypt and only Aaron's descendants could be priests from that time forward. Mary and Elizabeth were cousins, they both had the blood of Aaron in their veins and therefore John the Baptist and Jesus were both qualified to be priests; they were descendants of Aaron, the brother of Moses.

John the Baptist had Levitical blood from both his mother and his father, he was born to train disciples to follow Jesus. Essentially John the Baptist's work was finished once Jesus's ministry began.

Jesus Christ was the "Yahweh Elohim" (Hebrew) known in English as "Lord God" who did the creating in Genesis chapter one. He apparently shared the Godhead, with the one Who became the Father when Jesus divested Himself of His divinity and became born in the flesh and there is no trinity.

There was no God the Father and no God the Son until this miraculous conception occurred in Matthew 1:20 NKJ - **20** But while he thought about these things, behold, an angel of the Lord appeared to him in a dream, saying, "Joseph, son of David, do not be afraid to take to you Mary your wife, for that which is conceived in her is of the Holy Spirit".

The Holy Spirit is the intrinsic nature and power of God. There was just the two entities of the Godhead each distinct and self-contained. They were both equally God. They were the Elohim in the Hebrew of the Old Testament.

John 1:1 thru 4 MKJ - **1** In the beginning was the Word (Christ), and the Word was with God, and the Word was God. **2** He was in the beginning with God. **3** All things were made through Him, and without Him nothing was made that was made. **4** In Him was life, and the life was the light of men.

Jesus Christ was the God that killed all the firstborn in Egypt and He led Moses out of Egypt and into the promised land; the children of Israel followed Moses. For clarification Christ was in a pillar of fire by night and He was in a pillar of a cloud by day; Moses followed Christ.

Exodus 12:29,51 NKJ - **29** And it came to pass at midnight that the LORD struck all the firstborn in the land of Egypt, from the firstborn of Pharaoh who sat on his throne to the firstborn of the captive who *was* in the dungeon, and all the firstborn of livestock. **51** And it came to pass, on that very same day, that the LORD brought the children of Israel out of the land of Egypt according to their armies.

The LORD GOD was also the spokesman at the Godhead as explained previously from the gospel of John chapter one. He was the Creator, all things were made by Him, and He divested Himself of His divinity to become Jesus Christ, the Saviour of mankind.

During the Council of Trent, Nicolaus, Constantine, and the other religious leaders devised a church government, which included the Nicene Creed, (doctrine of Trinity), and was patterned after the Roman and Babylonian civil governments, which were ruled by a monarch. The "church" leader, (the pope), was given power over the people in the same way a governor has civil authority over the people.

THE PRIESTHOOD OF JESUS CHRIST

It is important to keep in mind that Jesus Christ was in a priestly order above Levi, son of Jacob. Jesus was of the order of Melchizedek priest of the MOST HIGH GOD; part of the spiritual Godhead and not an earthly priesthood.

NOTE: The earthly priesthood lineage of Jesus Christ came down from Simon the Just and was crossed into the royal kingly line descending from King David through his son, Nathan.

NOTE: The marriage of Mattathiah and the daughter of Simon the Just, a Priest, brings the priestly line into the genealogy of Jesus Christ.

NOTE: Heli was the father of Mary and he was the older brother of Joseph of Arimathea. Heli and Joseph of Arimathea were Levites with mixed blood, the royal line which came down from King David and a priestly line which came down from Aaron the High Priest.

NOTE: Anna a Levite was the daughter of Joseph of Arimathea. Salome, a Levite the wife of Zebedee and mother of James and John (Matthew 27:56) and probably the sister of Mary, the mother of our Lord (John 19:25). James and John are said to be first cousins of Jesus and their mother, Salome was Jesus' aunt (Matthew 20:20).

Salome sought for her sons places of honor in Christ's kingdom (Matthew 20:21, compare 19:28) and she witnessed the crucifixion (Mark 15:40) and was present with the other women at the sepulcher (Matthew 27:56).

NOTE: The Royal House of Britain an enduring Dynasty, written by Rev. W. M. H. Milner M.A. – Fifteenth Edition "The Covenant Publishing Co. LTD. 8 Blades Court, Deodar Road, Putney, London SW15 2NU"

TITHING

In the parable of the tax collector Jesus spoke of tithing in Luke 18:12 NKJ – (the Pharisee said), **12** I fast twice a week; I give tithes of all that I possess.' Hebrews 7:5 NKJ - **5** And indeed those who are of the sons of Levi, who receive the priesthood, have a commandment to receive tithes from the people according to the law, that is, from their brethren, though they have come from the loins of Abraham.

Some churches today believe that Jesus had no authority to demand that Christians tithe because tithes in the old covenant were collected by the Levites not realizing that Jesus actually had Levitical blood in his veins.

These same churches believe Jesus only taught alms giving which was a part of the beneficence of the church as written in Job 29:13 NKJ - **13** The blessing of a perishing *man* came upon me, and I caused the widow's heart to sing for joy (an example of Old Testament alms giving). We see by this that Job gave alms to the widows and orphans which was done in addition to tithing in the old covenant. The amount was voluntary and personal a New Testament example of alms giving, is in Matthew 6:1 thru 4.

Like so many other things in ancient Jewish society tithing is a foregone conclusion. Tithe is an old English word for tenth, this was a certain amount commanded by God. Abraham paid tithes to Melchisedek back before Israel or Levi ever existed. Hebrews 7:6,9 NKJ - **6** but he (Melchisedek) whose genealogy is not derived from them received tithes from Abraham and blessed him who had the promises. **9** Even Levi, who receives tithes, paid tithes through Abraham, so to speak.

The really important thing to remember here is that non-reluctant tithing from an attitude of love, giving and sharing and most of all obedience to God are what makes both tithing and alms successful.

Realizing that no church can operate without money, nor can they operate an orphan's and widow's program, nor can they feed the poor and destitute without the generosity of others. In a righteous society when the churches of our land organize and administer social welfare to the poor, to widows and to orphans; this should not be the assignment of our government.

Approximately 425 B.C. God was telling the Jews who had returned to Jerusalem from exile in Persia the following message in Malachi 3:6 thru 10 NKJ - **6** "For I *am* the LORD, I do not change; therefore you are not consumed, O sons of Jacob. **7** Yet from the days of your fathers you have gone away from My ordinances and have not kept *them.* Return to Me, and I will return to you," Says the LORD of hosts. "But you said, 'In what way shall we return?' **8** "Will a man rob God? Yet you have robbed Me! But you say, 'In what way have we robbed You?' In tithes and offerings. **9** You are cursed with a curse, for you have robbed Me, *even* this whole nation. **10** Bring all the tithes into the storehouse, that there may be food in My house, and try Me now in this," says the LORD of hosts, "If I will not open for you the windows of heaven and pour out for you *such* blessing that *there will* not *be room* enough *to receive it.*

In short the message was "give from the heart and your gift will be multiplied" Luke 6:38 NKJ – (Jesus said), **38** "Give, and it will be given to you: good measure, pressed down, shaken together, and running over will be put into your bosom. For with the same measure that you use, it will be measured back to you."

Any church where the Pastor has to badger, beg or plead with the congregation for sufficient funds to operate on should close the doors, lock it up and go home.

It's so obvious that people who do not support their church in an affluent society are not seeking God, they are attending for their own personal wrong reasons and all the preaching you could do will probably not change their attitude.

Usually people who assemble with others to really worship God and support the congregation in its outreach program who voluntarily tithe and give offerings are people who get the breaks in life.

When some families first begin to attend Church they are driving an old clunker and they are not well dressed but in a couple of years that all changes for the better when they are faithful givers. God is not sleeping, He rewards those who are diligent in obeying Him. Obedience is proof to Him as we are showing our love for Him. 2 Corinthians 9:7 NKJ - *7 So let* each one *give* as he purposes in his heart, not grudgingly or of necessity; for God loves a cheerful giver (the husband sets the example for the family.)

CHAPTER ELEVEN
TRUE WOMANHOOD REALLY MATTERS

HAS TRUE WOMANHOOD BEEN LOST?

The scene in the garden of Eden was a beautiful semi-tropical veritable paradise.

The young man (Adam) in the picture seemed to have everything going for him; he had perfect health, radiant good looks and a keen alert mind. His employment was ideal, attending the garden with every abundant wealth in natural resources nearby. A paradise? Yes!

Adam undoubtedly walked and talked with the LORD God every day and as he walked in these gorgeous surroundings, he ate the delectable natural fruits, he observed and petted the animals; all the animals were friendly.

However an aching, gnawing feeling began to grow inside of him. He was not content, he was lonesome for one of his kind, someone to talk to with whom he could share the beauty of the garden, as well as his plans, hopes, and dreams. He also realized that all of the animals had a mate of their own kind, but he did not! He was alone!

WHY WOMAN WAS CREATED

Genesis 2:18, 22-24 NKJ - **18** *And the LORD God said, "It is not good that man should be alone; I will make him a helper comparable to him."* **22** *Then the rib which the LORD God had taken from man He made into a woman, and He brought her to the man.* **23** *And Adam said: "This is now bone of my bones and flesh of my flesh; she shall be called woman, because she was taken out of man."* **24** *Therefore a man shall leave his father and mother and be joined to his wife, and they shall become one flesh.*

Scripture tells us what a woman should be in Proverbs 31:10-31 NKJ **10** *Who can find a virtuous wife? For her worth is far above rubies.* **11** *The heart of her husband safely trusts her; so he will have no lack of gain.* **12** *She does him good and not evil all the days of her life.* **13** *She seeks wool and flax, and willingly works with her hands.* **14** *She is like the merchant ships, she brings her food from afar.* **15** *She also rises while it is yet night, and provides food for her household, and a portion for her maidservants.* **16** *She considers a field and buys it; from her profits she plants a vineyard.* **17** *She girds herself with strength, and strengthens her arms.* **18** *She perceives that her merchandise is good, and her lamp does not go out by night.* **19** *She stretches out her hands to the distaff, and her hand holds the spindle.* **20** *She extends her hand to the poor, yes, she reaches out her hands to the needy.* **21** *She is not afraid of snow for her household, for all her household is clothed with scarlet.* **22** *She makes tapestry for herself; her clothing is fine linen and purple.* **23** *Her husband is* *known in the gates, when he sits among the elders of the land. ²⁴ She makes linen garments and sells them, and supplies sashes for the merchants. ²⁵ Strength and honor are her clothing; she shall rejoice in time to come. ²⁶ She opens her mouth with wisdom, and on her tongue is the law of kindness. ²⁷ She watches over the ways of her household, and does not eat the bread of idleness. ²⁸ Her children rise up and call her blessed; her husband also, and he praises her: ²⁹ "Many daughters have done well, but you excel them all." ³⁰ Charm is deceitful and beauty is passing, but a woman who fears the LORD, she shall be praised. ³¹ Give her of the fruit of her hands, and let her own works praise her in the gates.*

As we watch the societies of the world we can see it would be a happier place for all if every young girl would be taught this inspired account of her reason for being and if every young boy of today could be given proper understanding of becoming a future husband and a father.

God's instructions for the young and the old in Titus 2:1 thru 5 NKJ - **1** But as for you, speak the things which are proper for sound doctrine: **2** that the older men be sober, reverent, temperate, sound in faith, in love, in patience; **3** the older women likewise, that they be reverent in behavior, not slanderers, not given to much wine, teachers of good things-- **4** that they admonish the young women to love their husbands, to love their children, **5** to be discreet, chaste, homemakers, good, obedient to their own husbands, that the <u>word of God may not be blasphemed</u>.

WOMEN HAVE QUESTIONS, GOD HAS THE ANSWERS

*What feminine characteristics should a woman have?
*Just where do women fit in, anyway?
*What value does the Creator place on women?
*What is the purpose of a woman?

The personalities of many modern women today have the tendency to be aggressive, domineering, loudmouthed, and "hard" in their approach to life, causing a distressing phenomenon. First of all it seems to make life for her more distressing, for her family and for everyone else. An obvious sign of distress are ulcers, formerly thought of as an essentially male illness. Ulcers are now afflicting almost as many women as men, especially women in the business and executive fields. The more women stray into the male areas of life, the more health issues they have such as high blood pressure, heart disease, and other similar maladies tend to be their lot as well.

God has designed women <u>for a purpose</u> and <u>with a purpose</u>. Women hurt themselves competing against males, with other women and even themselves, they admit their frustrations and emptiness and have deep problems that are mental, spiritual and emotional.

Far too many women around the world have been brainwashed into believing it is beneath their intellectual station to be a housewife, homemaker and a mother.

Question, what do you suppose is the most gratifying moment in a woman's life? Perhaps when she holds her first baby in her arms? Or when her husband first proposed to her? Maybe it is the work place where she got her first job or when she won her first big business deal, or received a job promotion.

Obviously men are not self-sufficient, they get lonely, and they need help for many reasons! Man is not complete unto himself, every man needs inspiration, warmth, and balance imparted by the right woman as his wife at his side!

Man could never achieve the full, abundant, peaceful, balanced life which God intended for him without the help of his woman.

In Genesis 2:18 NKJ. **18** And the LORD God said, "*It is* not good that man should be alone; I will make him a helper comparable to him."

God created woman to share with her man his life, plans, hopes and dreams. She was created specifically to help him, to be his helpmate!

Many women become edgy, resentful, and frustrated, heading up a "blind alley" as they are failing to fulfill the very purpose for which they were created! A wife needs to learn to be responsive to her husband, helping him with his plans regarding the home, share with him fun-times and together they are preparing a way of life for the family's future.

A woman needs to realize she plays a big part in the success of her husband; his triumphs and achievements are partly her own as well. And just as important she should equally share in his sorrow and disappointments, giving him the right kind of balance along with positive support, encouragement and contentment.

A very important area for a woman to cultivate success and her service is that of bearing and training the children. Certainly young mothers exert a powerful influence on the leaders of tomorrow! Teaching her children is far more important than any office position. A woman also needs to realize the overwhelming importance of zealously and joyously dedicating herself to this as their highest physical calling. Parents are responsible for the spiritual life of their children. Proverbs 22:6 NKJ **6** Train up a child in the way he should go, and when he is old he will not depart from it.

Christian women who objectively and enthusiastically give themselves to their God given calling are adding immeasurably to their own happiness and well-being and that of their family members. Putting God first goes a long way, it is very deep and far reaching as well as adding to the entire society in which we all live.

It cannot be said loud enough or often enough that women actually accomplish far more in the end by being the kind of wife and mother that God Almighty intended.

Abraham Lincoln the most revered of all American Presidents at the height of his accomplishments stated: "All that I am or ever hope to be I owe to my angel mother." His mother was a great example of a dedicated mother and a witness for God. She was familiar with much and had the wisdom God had given to her as she gave her son teachings such as patient teachings, religious instructions, guidance, encouragement, inspiration and wisdom too.

THE ULTIMATE GOAL

To the woman who reads and understands the Bible, another goal presents itself. The goal of preparing to help rule and construct society in the world of tomorrow as it states in Revelation 2:26 and 5:10 NKJ (Jesus said), **26 And he who overcomes, and keeps My works until the end, to him I will give power over the nations--** 10 And have made us kings and priests to our God; and we shall reign on the earth."

Today many women are leading and directing businesses, they are busy with the family in addition to public activities, they are learning and preparing for tomorrow's world, alongside of their husbands. But, "Can every woman be this multitasked"? The answer is "probably not"!

A woman needs to develop her natural talents given to her by God. She needs to be aware of the opportunities around her to excel as a wife and a mother as these goals are often ignored. To be successful an early education is extremely important and should not be overlooked. Her husband and her children rely on her every day and will continue to do so into the future.

Every man, woman and child are responsible to others in various ways, in the family, the community and socially in general.

When the wife is home she learns to be zealous and wise in her planning, executing and following through regarding her domestic responsibilities. She knows and understands how to plan and delegate. She is the CEO over her children, caring, training and watching. Her day does not end when the sun goes down, other duties outside of the home are also to be considered. She and her husband are training and preparing their children together for a successful, well-prepared life toward the Kingdom of God.

For both the husband and the wife, it is important to realize a basic principle of leadership. You must first learn how to responsively <u>take orders</u> and to <u>accomplish</u> <u>an assigned job</u> effectively, before you can be trusted with leadership. Jesus inspired the words in Acts 20:35 NKJ - *[35] I have shown you in every way, by laboring like this, that you must support the weak.*

Also remember the words of the Lord Jesus saying, **'It is more blessed to give than to receive.'** Women learn in a direct, personal sense to give in yielding, to be responsive, to help and to serve.

Happiness, joy, the sense of a deep-down satisfaction and accomplishment which comes to a dedicated and a successful wife and mother bears eloquent testimony to the eternal truth of the above inspired statement from the Son of God.

True femininity is much more than an attitude, it's an entire way of life! A woman's attitude and approach is basic, trying to help and add to the stature of her husband. Femininity is gladly bearing and training her children, spending time and effort with them in the realization that they may be the leaders of tomorrow. It is also, preparing herself for the ultimate spiritual goal in the Kingdom of God by learning the lessons of love, obedience and service here in this life and expressing these to the full as a wife and mother, while passing them on to the next generation. What an awesome responsibility!

It really matters to ask God for help; attempt to live in a Godly relationship with your husband, family and your society. Attempt to help, supplement, and serve in these areas to permeate your thinking and every approach to any situation, this brings balance to every decision in life.

Study, analyze and obey God's inspired instruction found in I Peter 3:1 thru 11 NKJ - *[1] Wives, likewise, be submissive to your own husbands, that even if some do not obey the word, they, without a word, may be won by the conduct of their wives, [2] when they observe your chaste conduct accompanied by fear. [3] Do not let your adornment be merely outward--arranging the hair, wearing gold, or putting on fine apparel-- [4] rather let it be the hidden person of the heart, with the incorruptible beauty of a gentle and quiet spirit, which is very precious in the sight of God.*

⁵ For in this manner, in former times, the holy women who trusted in God also adorned themselves, being submissive to their own husbands, ⁶ as Sarah obeyed Abraham, calling him lord, whose daughters you are if you do good and are not afraid with any terror. ⁷ Husbands, likewise, dwell with them with understanding, giving honor to the wife, as to the weaker vessel, and as being heirs together of the grace of life, that your prayers may not be hindered. ⁸ Finally, all of you be of one mind, having compassion for one another; love as brothers, be tenderhearted, be courteous; ⁹ not returning evil for evil or reviling for reviling, but on the contrary blessing, knowing that you were called to this, that you may inherit a blessing. ¹⁰ For "He who would love life and see good days, let him refrain his tongue from evil, and his lips from speaking deceit. ¹¹ Let him turn away from evil and do good; let him seek peace and pursue it.

With the attitude of deep respect for her husband, the wife will anticipate his wishes and his directions. The husband in turn will protect her, provide for her, love her and be the one on whom she can lean on and trust the rest of her natural life.

I Peter 3:7,8 NKJ *⁷ Husbands, likewise, dwell with them with understanding, giving honor to the wife, as to the weaker vessel, and as being heirs together of the grace of life, that your prayers may not be hindered. ⁸ Finally, all of you be of one mind, having compassion for one another; love as brothers, be tenderhearted, be courteous.*

One eminent physician has said that words like, "I am sorry, dear" for example are very medicinal in their effect in people's lives. A simple and sincere apology often averts a great deal of trouble. It takes courage to admit that you, and sometimes you alone, are wrong in a particular situation. Proverbs 15:1 NKJ - *[1] A soft answer turns away wrath, but a harsh word stirs up anger.*

A good thing to remember is if your husband is not a Christian, God says that he may be won apart from the word, or Bible teaching, by the conduct of the wife. If a wife shows deep respect and reverence for her husband, he may be won over to Christ by his admiration of her willingness to take the place which God has assigned the woman in his life. She wins him not by preaching at him, but by her Christian humility in submitting to him in her attitude of a life reflecting a meek and a quiet spirit.

In seeking to implement and magnify a feminine approach to life, let us consider **five** specific feminine characteristics which every woman would benefit from if she learns to apply them.

#1 Responsiveness and Service

Perhaps the most outstanding characteristic of a truly feminine woman is that of being warm and responsive to her husband. God created a woman to share a man's life, to love him, to respond to him and encourage him. God honors and blesses the institute of marriage. To honor God treat your husband the same way you want to be treated.

Together the wife and the husband should constantly attempt to make the home cleaner, more attractive and a happier place for the entire family as well as attempting to inspire the same thing in the lives of the children and other people.

An important question that should be considered is should a woman have a job outside of the home? The answer is neither a yes nor a no because all situations are different. Before the children come along this question may not be as critical but a person can only do a good job if they are not spread out too thin.

By reading Proverbs 31:10 thru 31 again may answer some questions for you.

Pray to God for wisdom and ask Him to help you make good and wise choices. Before trying it figure out together how this will affect your relationship with your husband and your children.

Some time ago, the U.S. News and World Report magazine ran an article captioned: "Does It Really Pay for the Wife to Work?" They pointed out that their added income provided by the wife's job was taken up with travel expenses, outside lunches, clothes, baby sitters fees etc. The article showed a family will gain very little.

#2 Tenderness and Beauty

A wise and happy wife wants her husband to be the head of her home. This happy woman can lean on him, she has a deep softness and tenderness for him.

This tender, yielding, serving state of mind automatically gives such a woman added beauty, a sparkle in her eyes and the capacity for patience, love, and compassion. She will be attractive and feminine with her manner of dress, her hair, and the way she conducts herself. She looks after her husband and children with much care.

Ephesians 5:22-24 NKJ - **22** Wives, submit to your own husbands, as to the Lord. **23** For the husband is head of the wife, as also Christ is head of the church; and He is the Savior of the body. **24** Therefore, just as the church is subject to Christ, so *let* the wives *be* to their own husbands in everything. (In this verse the wives are commanded to "submit" to their own husbands "as unto the Lord".)

A wise woman respects and admires her husband, she is his right arm so to speak. In the area of tenderness and beauty, a wise woman will give priority to true womanhood in every way possible. She will keep herself, her home, her husband and children neat and clean every day to make it comfortable for all that dwell inside the home.

#3 Intelligence and Understanding

"My education has prepared me to do more than have babies, change diapers, and clean the house!" That is true, the times of the day have taught women to forsake the God given role in her life for which she was created.

The woman is designed by God physically, mentally, and emotionally! The life on the fast track can be a whirlwind that at some point the woman had decided to experiment with. Will she someday regret this decision? A woman that has the role of being a wife, mother, and career minded, is totally overbooked. She has too much on her plate, something has to give, and probably it will be her home and family that begins to be neglected. As the saying goes, "you can't have it all!" Should a wife lose her husband later on and have to raise her children alone, she will have her education to fall back on.

A married woman needs sparkling intelligence and deep understanding. For she needs to perceive in a very special way how to complement and inspire her husband to accomplish the greatest possible success commensurate with his health, abilities, education and situation in life.

The main ingredient for a wife and mother is a kind, loving, dedicated attitude, and to possess a willing heart.

#4 Christian Virtue

Women need a continuing interest and self-esteem for themselves and to be good examples of decency, purity and virtue.

Proverbs 12:4 NKJ states: *4 An excellent wife is the crown of her husband, but she who causes shame is like rottenness in his bones.*

The entire family reaps the benefits of a happy home. A wife that loves her husband and has implicit trust from him and demonstrates her faithfulness and her loyalty to him is an example their children will remember for a life time. In turn, the husband and wife set a trend, a Christian principle, for generations to come. The diligent teaching and training will leave an everlasting impression upon the children.

A woman's example of virtue and decency will head off immeasurable heartache for her descendants for centuries to come as her children and grandchildren remember her legacy.

#5 Faith, hope and courage

A woman who shows faith in God, faith in her husband, and faith in herself is priceless. She is good for her husband and inspiring for her children. She manages a home of high accomplishments for her husband and children. Such a woman shows faith and hope, and trust in God.

There may come a time when her husband may be sick, absent or perhaps has died and she will have to carry on with courage and implicit faith. God will help her do her part to act in a feminine way for the future and wellbeing of the children.

In this area of life, especially to be truly and everlastingly feminine, a woman needs to believe in the true God. She needs to know, and understand that the great God of heaven stands behind the living laws he has set in motion and will bless, guide, and protect her, in her place as a woman as she yields to Him!

In Summary

What a much better place this world would be if all women were as God intended!

Then all husbands would have wives, partners, sweethearts and loving helpers that are for real, to assist them, buoy them up and share in the highest degree their hopes, dreams, and successes. <u>Marriage is designed by God to be taken seriously</u>!

Women play a big role in developing a better world today and a greater world tomorrow. What really matters and is important to remember is the truth of an old saying "The hand that rocks the cradle rules the world".

CHAPTER TWELVE
ARE MEN FULFILLING THEIR RESPONSIBILITIES?

A WELL BALANCED SOCIETY

Most Americans want to live in a nice quiet neighborhood where the good schools are located, where they have easy access to church and shops and they desire an easy commute to the work place. Everyone agrees that this is very desirable and for many Americans it works out just that way. Their children seem to be happy, well-adjusted and contented.

Why do some children grow up under such undesirable circumstances where there is no contentment to be found in the home? Why do some families live in an undesirable frame of mind? The answers are because of the failure in the family structure. All of man's ideas to improve on the family arrangement designed by God are not working.

There is an old saying, "Contentment makes poor men rich but discontentment makes rich men poor". When we look at the life of a man we automatically begin to wonder what are the things that really matter to him and to his family? Certainly contentment is high on the list if not the highest that really matters to most people.

But the question is how to achieve this goal in our own life and then how to keep it as it can be elusive.

Nothing in life is free especially in the pursuit of contentment. As we have seen Adam was able to receive contentment but it cost him a rib, he had to give up something to gain something.

According to Vines Complete Bible Dictionary, content can be a verb, a noun or an adjective. As a verb it primarily signifies "to be sufficient, to be strong, possess sufficient strength, to be enough for a thing, to be satisfied, contented with."

We have been shown in the book of Genesis how Adam was not content, he was lonely and his life was not complete even though he lived in the most beautiful perfect spot on earth, he had perfect climate and every imaginable type of food to eat such as fruit, nuts and vegetables.

Adam was surrounded by every animal and fowl that was created by God and he was not threatened by their presence and they were not in any danger either. God gave Adam the job of naming each and every creature.

Hebrews 13:5 NKJ - *5 Let your* conduct *be* without covetousness; *be* content with such things as you have. For He Himself has said, *"I will never leave you nor forsake you."*

Philippians 4:11 NKJ - **11** Not that I speak in regard to need, for I have learned in whatever state I am, to be content.

Genesis 2:20 NKJ - **20** So Adam gave names to all cattle, to the birds of the air, and to every beast of the field. But for Adam there was not found a helper comparable to him. (Adam was not content by himself).

I Timothy 6:6 NKJ - **6** Now godliness with contentment is great gain.

(The Bible is telling us that contentment is a learning process and a state of mind).

Another question is what does it mean to be godly? Godly means to be devout, which means to be cautious, careful as to the realization of the presence and claims of God, holding only God in reverence.

God gave us instructions to husbands as well as to wives and their responsibilities are different but just as important to the things that really matter in a marriage.

At the end of a long day the husband really needs a quiet peaceful oasis to come to where peace, love and joy are in abundance. A man needs a little time to relax and let his head clear from all he puts up with on the job all day long. A single man does not have this oasis; a married man does not have this oasis either if he comes home with a disgruntled attitude and starts yelling at the children and scolding his wife.

IMPORTANT THINGS THAT REALLY MATTER

Contentment needs to be learned by each person involved as it cannot survive under adverse circumstances.

In the home where the wife is a stay at home mom she should be prepared for her husband to arrive home from work and she should set the stage for the evening to be a pleasant one for him and the children.

A good suggestion for the wife might be to have the kids down for a nap before Dad gets home, a fresh cup of coffee and a cookie ready when he comes through the door to tide him over while the evening meal is being prepared and on the table.

Perhaps Dad could get the children up from their nap and play a while until the meal is on the table and everyone gets seated; then Dad would offer thanks for the food that God has provided.

Meal time is a time for family conversation, discussion and planning things for the next day. This is how contentment is formed, formed by a family being together, learning about each other and enjoying each other's company.

Understanding that things will come along to interfere with a day's planning but remember tomorrow will bring us back on schedule.

Dad plays an important part by taking charge on those days', things can get out of their regular routine but he reassures the family that everything is going to be alright. Dad plays a big part, by example, in teaching the children how to become good parents themselves!

Husbands and wives who have put these methods of operation into practice will tell you that planning things in life during child rearing really matters because the entire family benefits.

God has commanded husbands to love their wives as Christ loves the Church and gave Himself for it. It would be good for us to review a few of the **ten** biblical tips we were given to enable us to live contented happy lives.

#1. We must realize first of all that Christ really did give up his earthly physical life for His church. We are His family, He expects nothing less from fathers and husbands than to love their wives and trust and respect them just as he loves, trusts and respects himself.

This is very important and it really matters! In Ephesians 5:25 NKJ [25] Husbands, love your wives, just as Christ also loved the church and gave Himself for it. With this frame of mind, the children are happy, the wife is happy and we all enjoy a happy contented household.

#2. In Ephesians 5:28 thru 33 NKJ - [28] So husbands ought to love their own wives as their own bodies; he who loves his wife loves himself. [29] For no one ever hated his own flesh, but nourishes and cherishes it, just as the Lord *does* the church. [30] For we are members of His body, of His flesh and of His bones.

31 *"For this reason a man shall leave his father and mother and be joined to his wife, and the two shall become one flesh."* **32** This is a great mystery, but I speak concerning Christ and the church. **33** Nevertheless let each one of you in particular so love his own wife as himself, and let the wife *see* that she respects *her* husband.

#3. Sometimes when your wife is not feeling well, show respect and do not create unnecessary noises in the house, loud music or TV, be available to render her aid. She may need a couple of hours of bed rest so keep the children occupied and quiet. Probably checking on her from time to time would also be appreciated.

Remembering to ask God to help you understand her needs and to show you ways to be more considerate and your wife will love you for it.

#4. Remembering to be tender hearted and kind is always a plus, never to be harsh with her or the children. Remember they are God's gift to you, be thankful always for them. Life would be very lonely without your mate so being careful not to use irritated tones of voice or to be impatient really matters.

#5. Always remember no married man should look at another woman lustfully; his wife probably would appreciate some thoughtfulness along with a compliment or two as she would love the attention.

Jesus Christ warned us that a married man who looks upon a woman to lust after her has committed adultery with her already in his heart, this really matters. Matthews 5:28 NKJ – (Jesus said) **28 But I say to you that whoever looks at a woman to lust for her has already committed adultery with her in his heart.**

James 4:4 NKJ - **4** Adulterers and adulteresses! Do you not know that friendship with the world is enmity with God? Whoever therefore wants to be a friend of the world makes himself an enemy of God.

#6. A truly Christian woman is a modest woman who behaves in the manner of a lady. Her hair style, her clothing, her manners reflect her inner self, her character. This type of woman is a jewel of great price and brings a great sense of pride to her husband. A husband who is worthy of his salt so to speak will let her know how much he appreciates her and how proud he is that she is his wife. Men should treat their wife the way they would want to be treated as this really matters.

I Timothy 2:9, 10 NKJ - **9** in like manner also, that the women adorn themselves in modest apparel, with propriety and moderation, not with braided hair or gold or pearls or costly clothing, **10** but, which is proper for women professing godliness, with good works.

#7. Husbands must be very careful not to compare the way your wife looks or compare her beauty to other women and the way they look. If other women turn your head when you are with your wife don't think she hasn't noticed and what will she think you do when she isn't with you. It is very important and it really matters the way a husband acts toward his mate as he can hurt her emotionally and spiritually.

#8. Remember when you and your wife were dating? Continue to build her up, give her self-esteem, brag on her. Let her know she is the greatest woman on earth! Praise her and compliment her for diligently tending to the home and to your needs and the needs of the children. Women love being acknowledged and appreciated as much as men do and perhaps a little more. Keeping this in mind is a priority and you will be adequately rewarded by a very happy woman.

#9. Make a practice of reading in your Bible, the book of "Song of Solomon" every now and again. This may sharpen your mind to see things in your wife you may be taking for granted. Never criticize or make fun of any part of her body. If you see a flaw she knows it is there and she may be self-conscious already besides what would it benefit to humiliate her and lose favor with her? Your wife will feel enamored and delighted if you show her proper appreciation for the way she looks. There is a time to speak and there is a time to be quiet as this really matters.

#10. The Bible says a virtuous woman is a jewel of great price and where your treasure is, there will your heart be also. Keep the romance alive in your relationship with your wife in your marriage. Your marriage will reap huge benefits if you do and will last a lifetime.

Let your wife always be the apple of your eye. Give her genuine interest and listen intently when you are conversing let her know she is the most important person in your life and she needs to be reassured regularly.

A good wife is a tremendous blessing from God so be thankful daily to Him for giving you this person to spend your life with; this is something that really does matter.

To have the best of happiness and abundant living is to trust in God, have trust in your mate, love and appreciate everyone in your family and sphere of friends. You will prosper, you will have a happy home, and you will have a lot of friends. These are all things that really matter!

To be a good husband and a leader of the home takes work! Contentment takes time, it takes wisdom and the desire to serve God first, then your family, then yourself.

We look forward to the day when the home will be as God designed it to be for every household of every community on earth involving every race of people. This future time is when Christ returns and we will sing "peace on earth and good will among men and women", when the earth is populated with people who have love toward each other as Jesus said in Matthew 22:37 thru 39 NKJ - **37** Jesus said to him, **"'You shall love the LORD your God with all your heart, with all your soul, and with all your mind.' 38 This is the first and great commandment. 39 And the**

second *is* like it: 'You shall love your neighbor *(your wife is your closest neighbor)* **as yourself.** (This is the ultimate contentment).

Jesus referred to His church as a woman and the woman needs a leader that is the way it was designed by God. God has commissioned married men to be the head of their household, the command is to lead and rule in love not to be a dictator and not slack in their responsibilities.

Ephesians 5:23, 33 NKJ - **23** For the husband is head of the wife, as also Christ is head of the church; and He is the Savior of the body. **33** Nevertheless let each one of you in particular so love his own wife as himself, and let the wife *see* that she respects *her* husband.

The Apostle Paul in his letter to the Church at Corinth wrote the following concerning the Church. 2 Corinthians 11:2 NKJ - **2** For I am jealous for you with godly jealousy. For I have betrothed you to one husband, that I may present *you as* a chaste virgin to Christ.

Every one of these are important factors that really matter!

CHAPTER THIRTEEN
SUCCESSFUL CHILD REARING

Usually in the first year of a marriage a young couple spend most of their leisure time bonding. They may enjoy walking, biking, swimming, attend ball games, movie theatre and concerts, just anything that they enjoy to do and can afford, something they do together.

At some point nature will take its course and morning sickness will be followed by a trip to the doctor and reveal they are beginning to have a larger family. This is a time for a young couple like no other, the feelings and emotions will send chill bumps all the way up the spine to the top of their heads.

The feelings of elation and joy sweep over them but then they get quiet and mirth gives way to still sobriety as the awesome seriousness of this new responsibility starts to sink in.

There is no doubt that this gift from God will one day soon be cradled in your arms.

It is a delightful and amusing sight to watch new parents as they stand by a baby crib with their faces all aglow staring at this new little person that is a part of them both.

They watch the fingers and toes as they move, they see the dimples in the cheeks or chin. The arch of the eyebrows, the hairline, the nose as they look for similarities to either of their families. The gene pools of two families have come together in this one little person who's DNA can be traced back through family lines for hundreds of years.

Now the seriousness of how to get this child safely from the cradle to adulthood begins to take over the minds of the parents as there are myriads of things to be on guard about but the scariest things are childhood diseases. Today there are dozens of ailments affecting children that may have never been heard of by the average person.

Healthy children are important but physical health is only part of the equation. There exists today a dark cloud over the health of a child in regard to medicines that are given to expectant mothers.

Many of the psychological problems in children today are believed to have begun at the doctor's office when the mother began taking prescription drugs while she was expecting. Autism is one hotly debated disease topic in regard to prenatal medications which may or may not be true. The medical profession wants us to believe that they can cure all ills and that their kind of medicine fits all ills.

SCHOOL SHOOTINGS

The list of mass school shootings by students goes back to 1988 and even further. It is believed the problem points to the doctors for antidepressant prescription drugs for our children which are suspect in many mental health problems.

The Bible gives us the answer, as a nation are we ready to listen?

The very big mistake has been our nation has turned away from God. We told Him to get out of our schools, our government, our homes, our churches, our community, and our lives. This is happening all across our land so we must remember without God we are doomed!

Proverbs 13:17 NKJ - **17** A wicked messenger falls into trouble, but a faithful ambassador *brings* health.

Jeremiah 33:6 NKJ - **6** Behold, I will bring it health and healing; I will heal them and reveal to them the abundance of peace and truth.

3 John 1:2 NKJ - **2** Beloved, I pray that you may prosper in all things and be in health, just as your soul prospers.

God is telling us in His Word why so many of our children are sick and why our people are in poor health.

Our nation's sickness is an epidemic without a positive solution and our nation is dying.

People from all walks of life are having mental health problems and this includes some of our children.

From 1988 to 2016 accurate statistics of school shootings show 169 wounded and 79 killed, however a lot of information concerning these shootings has been kept from the public. That brings up another question, are the statisticians protecting the shooters, the parents, the doctors or the government?

CHILDHOOD ACCIDENTS

Accidents happen in childhood, despite your best childproofing and safety efforts. Here's a list of some common childhood emergencies and accidents and the places they're likely to happen.

Other serious concerns of new parents that need to be confronted, some short range, some long range and some fatal.

- **Burns**, are one of the most common childhood accidental injuries. These include sunburns, electrical burns, and burns caused by stoves, lamps, matches, lighted cigarettes, and fireplaces. Other dangers include hot liquids and steam from a pan, cup, or hot water heater. Burns from bathwater are also common,

especially if your water heater is set higher than 120 degrees Fahrenheit.
- **Poisoning** from ingesting medicines, shampoo, aftershave, perfume, vitamins, cleaning products, and from exposure to gas appliances such as stoves and heaters.
- **Drowning** is a leading cause of accidental death among children, and it can happen in bathtubs, toilets, buckets, swimming pools, and areas of open water.
- **Head injuries** caused by falls from highchairs, beds, furniture, stairs, slippery floors, and play equipment.
- **Choking** on food, toys, batteries, bottle caps, coins, balloons, or other small objects.
- **Strangulation** caused by necklaces, drawstrings on clothes, baby headbands, strings, ties, and ribbons as well as cords on toys, household appliances, window blinds, and other fixtures.
- **Nose injuries** caused by running into stationary objects, falling on a hard surface, or deflecting a flying toy (or the fist or foot of another child).
- **Items stuck in a nostril or ear**, like small stones, chewable vitamins, pebbles, and peas.
- **Cuts and scratches** caused by sharp fingernails (either your baby's own or some other child's), pets, sharp objects (like knives, appliances with blades, and glass or other breakables), sharp edges of furniture, and sticks and other pointed objects outside.
- **Fractures and sprains** caused by hard falls and, as your child enters the toddler years, by

playing energetically. Children tend to break bones more easily than adults because they have soft areas near the end of each bone called growth plates.
- **Contusions**—bruises under the skin—caused by bumps and falls.
- A **pulled elbow**, caused by picking up your child by one arm, jerking his arm forcefully, or swinging him around by the arms. The forearm bone can slip out of the elbow joint and sometimes slip back without medical attention.
- **Eye injuries** caused by dust, sand, chemical sprays, or other types of foreign matter in the child's eye.
- **Falls** from infant seats, highchairs, changing tables, walkers, and stairs.

Other serious concerns new parents need to be aware of, some short range, some long range and some fatal.

Places to watch out for:

- **Cribs**, which can be a risk for pinched fingers and limbs, strangulation (from crib toys that have string, cords, or ribbons), and suffocation under blankets and pillows. Drop rails can also suffocate and strangle, and crib bumpers are associated with SIDS (sudden infant death syndrome).
- **Cars** with improperly installed car seats, or when a child is accidentally left in a locked car, which causes dangerous overheating.

- **Windows**, which children can fall from or get strangled in cords.
- **Bathrooms**, which are the main places for slips on wet surfaces, bumps and scrapes on bathroom fixtures, and cuts from shaving devices. A baby can drown in an inch of water, so be vigilant when your child is in the bath and be sure to keep the toilet off limits (unless you're supervising).

All childhood accidents are things that really matter!

DISEASES OF BABY'S FIRST YEAR

Another very important thing that really matters is that regardless of the age of a new mother she must realize that her life from here will never be the same; if she herself is very young her adolescent days are over. A new mother has a new routine; she will be getting up at all hours of the night to change diapers, to nurse or fix bottles, to comfort the child when the baby cries. A baby cries for a valid reason and the child should never be ignored. There are more than a dozen diseases a baby can get besides the regular childhood diseases we have all heard about. A new mother should learn about these symptoms in order to monitor her little one. These infections are called neonatal and can occur from birth to one-year-old.

Further information: Neonatal infection

- meconium aspiration syndrome
- Group B streptoccus infection

- prenatal Listeria
- Ureaplasma urealyticum infection
- Cytomegalovirus
- Candidia albicans infection
- Candida parapsilosis infection
- respiratory Syncytial Virus infection
- metapneumovirus (HMPV) infection
- rhinovirus; common cold
- parainfluenza (PIV) infection
- human coronavirus infection
- respiratory distress syndrome

The most frightening disease of all is called 'SIDS', Sudden Infant Death Syndrome.

After a baby reaches the second year or older until school age they can still become a victim of nearly 50 other childhood diseases. It is easy to see that mothering is not a laid back job. A baby requires all of a parent's energy every minute, hour, week, month and year.

Keeping a list of all the diseases posted with the symptoms is a very wise and important thing to do, as this really matters.

Diseases of older children:

- AIDS
- Anemia
- Asthma
- Bronchiolitis
- Cancer
- Candidiasis ("Thrush")

IMPORTANT THINGS THAT REALLY MATTER

- Chagas disease
- Chickenpox
- Croup
- Cystic Fibrosis
- Cytomegalovirus (the virus most frequently transmitted before birth)
- dental caries
- Diabetes (Type 1)
- Diphtheria
- Duchenne muscular dystrophy
- Fifth disease
- Congenital Heart Disease
- Influenza
- Intussusception (medical disorder)
- Juvenile idiopathic arthritis
- Leukemia
- Measles
- Meningitis
- Molluscum contagiosum
- Mumps
- Nephrotic syndrome
- Osgood-Schlatter disease
- Osteogenesis Imperfecta (OI)
- Pneumonia
- Polio
- Rheumatic fever
- Rickets
- Roseola
- Rubella
- Sever's disease
- Tetanus
- Tuberculosis
- Volvulus
- Whooping cough

- <u>Hepatitis A</u>
- <u>Fever</u>
- <u>Scarlet fever</u> (Scarletina)
- <u>Mono</u>
- <u>Lyme Disease</u>
- <u>Xerophthalmia</u>
- <u>PANDAS</u>
- <u>PANS</u>

The symptoms of these diseases should be posted in plain sight and the mother should be aware of them.

TOBACCO

The last statistics available was in 2008, 46 million U.S. adults were smokers, that figures out to be approximately 20% of the population.

Percentage by race and ethnicity:
22 % of whites
21.3 % of blacks
15.8 % Hispanics
32.4 % of American and Alaskan natives
9.9 % of Asian Americans
23.7 % were in the 25 to 44 age group of all races

Smoking is the culprit in 9 out of 10 lung cancer deaths. Lung cancer is the number one killer in cancer deaths.

Even though smoking is a preventable cause it still remains the major cause of cancer mortality.

Figures from the CDC of 2008 are even truer today. Tobacco use is responsible for one in 5 deaths in the U.S.A.

Anyone smoking is committing suicide, as suicide is defined as someone intentionally taking their own life with no set degree or speed of action pertinent to the event. Suicide can be instant or it can take years depending upon the method used but in either case death is just as certain and death will last just as long. The word has been out and been published for 34 years that tobacco kills and it is no respecter of persons.

Anyone smoking who is aware of these facts are in denial and are lying to their own conscience!

Everyone who stubbornly insists on continuing to smoke should seriously consider the sixth commandment you are without excuse; death will be painful.

Deuteronomy 5:17 NKJ - [17] 'You shall not murder. (This includes yourself).

Any parent giving tobacco to their child should be convicted of crimes against children.

It is reported annually an average of 443,000 deaths occur in the U.S.A. relating to tobacco. There are many reasons; people who smoke have babies, they smoke at home and in their automobiles, children are breathing in second hand smoke, children become addicted before they can walk.

Before these children are in their teen years they are sneaking cigarettes out of their parents packs and smoking out behind the house or in the garage or in the yard behind a tree.

As far back as 1982 the United States Surgeon General's report cited smoking as the major single cause of death by cancer in the United States. It is just as true today! Cigarette smoking accounts for at least 30% of all cancer deaths. It is linked with an increased risk of the following cancers:

* lung
* larynx (voice box)
* oral cavity (mouth, tongue, and lips)
* pharynx (throat)
* esophagus (tube connecting the throat to the stomach)
* stomach
* pancreas
* cervix
* kidney
* bladder
* acute myeloid leukemia

Smoking is responsible for almost 9 out of 10 lung cancer deaths. Lung cancer is the leading cause of cancer death in both men and women, and is one of the hardest cancers to treat. Lung cancer is a disease that can often be prevented. Some religious groups that promote non-smoking as part of their religion are the Mormons and Seventh-day Adventists, and they have much lower rates of lung cancer and other smoking-related cancers.

CHAPTER FOURTEEN
ABORTION

There is an epidemic of unwed mothers in the U.S.A. these days and many of them are teenagers, many girls are too young, they are not mentally ready nor prepared to be mothers. In our country from January 1, 2016 to December 9, 2016, women have aborted 1,027,387 babies. Abortion is the number one killer ahead of heart disease and cancer, per Realtime death toll. Abortions through the government assisted program called Planned Parenthood which should be called "Planned Murder Legalized"; the U.S. government contributes 11 billion dollars coming from the taxpayers to subsidize this organization, according to the Huffington Post. This was your money and mine used to finance baby killing.

During the time of Adolf Hitler's entire career he was responsible for approximately 15 million deaths.

There is no telling how many babies have been slaughtered in the U.S.A. since 1973 when baby killing became legal. If we do the math calculating forty-three years with an average of 1.2 million abortions per year this puts the United States of America at approximately 51,600,000 babies killed; enough to populate a large city.

In the Bible located in Genesis 4:10 NKJ - **10** And He (God) said, "What have you done? The voice of your brother's blood cries out to Me from the ground.

Can you imagine the crying of 51,600,000 dying babies, and the number is climbing higher each day. From the U.S.A. alone the cries from our aborted babies are going up into the ears of God. Our nation is going to be punished, we will pay for this horrendous sin, judgment is coming on our land and we will not escape.

When you think of this mass murder on a worldwide scale it is too mind boggling to try and comprehend this evil act. This sin is so terrible that it is unbelievable and most people never give it a second thought, unless it has occurred in their own family. This is a great tragedy because when our nation goes down we all go down together; God hates the killing of babies!

There should be such a public outcry against abortion that the ears of every politician in Washington D.C. and every state capital would be burning, and it should be relentless. We should be using every form of social media in existence to pound and keep pounding on our evil leader's minds until they reverse this 43 years of a horrendous curse and purge it from our land. As we have seen for a long time that those in higher office are not willing to stop abortion so it is up to the people to make it happen. Abortion is something that really matters!

AMERICA DOOMED?

The average American no doubt goes from day to day tending to his or her routine rarely mindful of what is really happening in the world or even what is happening in their own city, state, or county.

This book is being written for the purpose of informing each and every individual who wants to know the mind-set of God and what is happening on the earth regarding God's principles as they are really important and they really matter.

This is not a book about religion, it is about life. According to Random House College Dictionary religion is a set of beliefs concerning the cause of nature and purpose of the universe, it involves deities and ritual observances. Every race in every country on earth has a set of beliefs of this sort.

The issues raised in this writing have been proven and documented from history; they are as old as wind driven snow and it has been around a long-long time. The oldest history known to man reaches back to the time on the earth when it was covered in water before man walked upon it.

We need principles in our lives to survive. Random House tells us that a principle is an accepted or professed rule of action or conduct guiding requirements, basic common sense, law or doctrine.

Things have been tried and proven to be both effective and beneficial in every category that has been raised in this book. Experience is not necessarily the best teacher but it is by far the most effective and long lasting. Experience can leave a person scarred or crippled for the remainder of their life.

An old saying of truth goes like this, "He who heeds not a warning shall live to regret it." A very important guide book, the Holy Bible, first penned between 1445 B.C. and 1405 B.C. was written for a new nation that was being established, the nation of Israel.

This new nation was to have the guidelines, they were to be an example to all people of all nations and they were to become a priestly nation. They were given written instructions on "How to" for every facet of their lives. They were going to be blessed as no other nation before them had been; and they were to have health, wealth and prosperity. The plan was that other nations would look at them and see what they had and would want to copy their way of life so they too could be blessed in the same way.

If this principle of an idea would have caught on, nation after nation would have followed in their footsteps and all of the Middle East up to today would have been dwelling together side by side in blissful peace.

However there was a stringent rule attached to blessing this nation! This pilot nation had to obey the God of Abraham, Isaac and Jacob and if they did they would be blessed more than any nation on earth. This is why the "book of books" was written so that every generation going forward, even way into the future, could read it, adopt its principles, obey its laws and whoever does they will be blessed abundantly.

It was the Lord God, Jesus Christ the Creator who dictated to Moses to write the book as they journeyed. Moses was more than a scribe, he also led the Israelites through the wilderness for 40 years and he was a prophet. When Moses died at 120 years of age Joshua brought Israel over the Jordan River into Canaan into their promised land.

Israel did not obey God, they failed many times and in many ways, over and over again after they were settled in their new land, the land of Israel. They came into the land in 1405 B.C. and were driven out in 722 B.C. exiled for their disobedience. They were taken to the land of Assyria, Turkey today around the Black Sea and the Caspian Sea.

After they were in Assyria, the Babylonians came over and defeated the Assyrians in 612 B.C. The Israelites were able to escape from the Babylonians so they migrated up the Danube River from the Black Sea area.

For centuries, 2,000 years, they were not identified, they were only known as the lost tribes of Israel.

This is the story about a people, about history and not about a religion. These people were given the most prestigious opportunity ever given to any people on earth and they did not and would not appreciate this opportunity enough to fulfill their part of the bargain. They wanted to be blessed but they did not want to play by the rules, so God took away the blessings and they lost their homeland.

These people were gone but not forgotten, God had made a covenant with Abraham and these were Abraham's descendants.

Genesis 15:5 NKJ - **5** Then He brought him (Abraham) outside and said, "Look now toward heaven, and count the stars if you are able to number them." And He said to him, "So shall your descendants be."

Genesis 13:16 NKJ - **16** And I will make your descendants as the dust of the earth; so that if a man could number the dust of the earth, *then* your descendants also could be numbered.

With God making a promise such as this to Abraham common sense should tell us that God would know where Abraham's descendants were down through all the years to this very day.

God would also see to it that the blessings conferred by Jacob on his sons under God's inspiration would someday come to pass and they have, but it is not being widely taught by churches yet; it is mostly left to individual histories not taught in schools.

Genesis 49:1 thru 27 NKJ - **1** And Jacob called his sons and said, "Gather together, that I may tell you what shall befall you in the last days: **2** "Gather together and hear, you sons of Jacob, and listen to Israel your father. **3** "Reuben, you are my firstborn, my might and the beginning of my strength, the excellency of dignity and the excellency of power. **4** Unstable as water, you shall not excel, because you went up to your father's bed; then you defiled *it*—He went up to my couch. **5** "Simeon and Levi *are* brothers; instruments of cruelty *are in* their dwelling place. **6** Let not my soul enter their council; let not my honor be united to their assembly; for in their anger they slew a man, and in their self-will they hamstrung an ox. **7** Cursed *be* their anger, for *it is* fierce; and their wrath, for it is cruel! I will divide them in Jacob and scatter them in Israel. **8** "Judah, you *are he* whom your brothers shall praise; your hand *shall be* on the neck of your enemies; your father's children shall bow down before you. **9** Judah *is* a lion's whelp; from the prey, my son, you have gone up. He bows down, he lies down as a lion; and as a lion, who shall rouse him? **10** The scepter shall not depart from Judah, nor a lawgiver from between his feet, until Shiloh comes; and to Him *shall be* the obedience of the people. **11** Binding his donkey to the vine, and his donkey's colt to the choice vine, he washed his garments in wine, and his clothes in the blood of grapes. **12** His eyes *are* darker than wine, and his teeth whiter than milk. **13** "Zebulun shall dwell by the haven of the sea; he *shall become* a haven for ships, and his border shall adjoin Sidon. **14** "Issachar is a strong donkey, lying down between two burdens; **15** He saw that rest *was* good, and that the land *was* pleasant; he bowed his shoulder to bear *a burden,* and became a band of slaves. **16** "Dan shall judge his people as one of the tribes of Israel. **17** Dan shall be a serpent by the way, a viper by the path, that bites the horse's heels so that its rider shall fall backward. **18** I have waited for your salvation, O LORD! **19** "Gad, a troop shall tramp upon him, but he shall triumph at last. **20** "Bread from Asher *shall be* rich, and he shall yield royal dainties. **21** "Naphtali *is* a deer let loose; he uses beautiful words. **22** "Joseph *is* a fruitful bough, a fruitful bough by a well; his branches run over the wall. **23** The archers have bitterly grieved him, shot *at him* and hated him. **24** But his bow remained in strength, and the arms of his hands were made strong by the hands of the Mighty *God* of Jacob (From there *is* the Shepherd, the Stone of Israel), **25** By the God of your father who will help you, and by the Almighty who will bless you *with* blessings of heaven above, blessings of the deep that lies beneath, blessings of the breasts and of the womb. **26** The blessings of your father have excelled the blessings of my ancestors, up to the utmost bound of the everlasting hills. They shall be on the head of Joseph, and on the crown of the head of him who was separate from his brothers. **27** "Benjamin is a ravenous wolf; in the morning he shall devour the prey, and at night he shall divide the spoil."

These are the blessings promised to Abraham's descendants; as they were divided up among Jacob's sons, the grandsons of Isaac.

The so called lost tribes of Israel were located in the 20th century by looking back over the last 2500 years of history and searching out the people, nations and tongues and then tracing the origins of those people back to Genesis 49, all the way to Egypt.

Several historians have now researched this and we now know beyond a shadow of a doubt where the modern day sons of Abraham, Isaac and Jacob are located. To those desiring this information we would suggest reading Steven Collins book, "The Lost Ten Tribes of Israel Found".

The only saving grace for modern Israel, the sons of Isaac is redemption if we are to avoid doom. We must return to the God of Jacob. We must remember the story of Jonah and how Assyria repented.

CHAPTER FIFTEEN
PEOPLE OF A NATION

The question at this point is how to reach the people of the U.S.A. today with this message, but not only this nation but how to reach all English speaking nations plus a few others who are also sons of Isaac or Anglo Saxons is a challenge.

Most of these nations are free democratic or republic societies and most are either Protestant or Catholic or both.

At this point we need to ask the question why did God banish Israel from the land of Canaan and send them into exile? It is plain and simple because of disobedience.

Since Israel proved they were not going to obey Him and represent Him before the other nations they had to leave their land, not willingly but by force of the Assyrians.

Another question to be asked here is: "What was the three worst sins the people committed to be removed and evicted from the Promised Land?" Answer: "For forsaking the Sabbath Day, God's annual Holy Days and killing babies".

Killing babies started when Solomon married women from the near-by nations of Moab and Ammon who worshiped the pagan deities called Chemosh and Molech which required them to sacrifice a baby to these pagan gods. It wasn't too long until the women of Israel began to follow this pagan ritual and pass their babies through the fire to be burned alive as sacrifices to these gods. Solomon allowed them to go out and sacrifice their babies.

This ritual was carried out on the rim of the canyon called the Valley of the sons of Hinnom. This is where the term Gehenna fire or Hell fire had its beginning.

The place was called Tophet; the word Tophet is an ancient Hebrew word meaning "drum". Solomon had built two idols there for his foreign wives. One was a statue of Molech and the other was a statue of Chemosh. The pagan priest would take the baby from the mother's arms and place it in the arms of the idol then an attendant would pull the lever and tip the baby over into the burning flames as the mother was escorted away.

The ceremony was accompanied by an ensemble of drums loud enough to keep the mother from hearing the screams of her dying child that had been thrown into the fire. The mothers were brainwashed into believing they would receive a special blessing and prosperity for their sacrifices. They were not allowed to see the baby dumped into the flames or allowed to hear its painful screams as the flames blistered its skin and turned its little body into a blackened cinder then to ash.

One thing we can be sure of is that God was witnessing the sacrifices and heard the cry of each and every baby.

1 Kings 11:33 NKJ - **33** because they have forsaken Me, and worshiped Ashtoreth the goddess of the Sidonians, Chemosh the god of the Moabites, and Milcom the god of the people of Ammon, and have not walked in My ways to do *what is* right in My eyes and *keep* My statutes and My judgments, as *did* his father David.

These were some of the reasons Israel was banished from their land. Solomon, the wisest king who ever lived had become an abject fool. Solomon had taken 700 wives and 300 concubines and these women turned his heart away from God.

1 Kings 11:1,2 NKJ - **1** But King Solomon loved many foreign women, as well as the daughter of Pharaoh: women of the Moabites, Ammonites, Edomites, Sidonians, *and* Hittites-- **2** from the nations of whom the LORD had said to the children of Israel, "You shall not intermarry with them, nor they with you. Surely they will turn away your hearts after their gods." Solomon clung to these in love.

Things continued to get worse for Israel, they started forsaking observance of God's Sabbath day. They also forsook the seven annual Sabbaths (Holy Days – festivals), these are clearly laid out in Leviticus 23. And they also forsook observance of the Passover.

God sent the Assyrians down and they deported Israel out of their land in three deportations, the last one was 722 B.C. They were taken as slaves to serve the Assyrians where they stayed for over 100 years until they began a gradual migration up the Danube River which is 1700 miles from the Black Sea up into the Alps. They traveled over several Countries that spoke the Gaelic language, on to the European side of the Alps from the Ukraine and Finland and down to France which was called Gaul at that time.

The question here that looms largely for America is this, in fact there are several questions we are going to set forth for readers of this book to answer for themselves. These questions are for all English speaking Countries.

What is the difference in the days of old when babies were passed through the fire to Molech and Chemosh compared to the gods of today as babies are being sacrificed for "convenience", "selfishness", "money" and "birth control".

Jeremiah 32:26,27,35 NKJ -**26** Then the word of the LORD came to Jeremiah, saying, **27** "Behold, I *am* the LORD, the God of all flesh. Is there anything too hard for Me? **35** And they built the high places of Baal which *are* in the Valley of the Son of Hinnom, to cause their sons and their daughters to pass through *the fire* to Molech, which I did not command them, nor did it come into My mind that they should do this abomination, to cause Judah to sin.'

Any alert thinking person will have to ask themselves, "How much longer will God allow this to go on before He intervenes? In the U.S.A. abortion has been going on legally for 43 years. When will He step in to stop this madness? How much longer until we are marched out of our country? When will we experience our trail of tears? Who will be our "Assyrian captors"?

Singling out the United States as just one modern day nation of Israelite descendants we will submit the following: An average of 1.2 million abortions are taking place annually in the U.S.A. Does God hear the silent little screams as these baby's little arms and legs are vacuumed off? Does God see their little skulls being crushed so they can be shoved through a garbage disposal or flushed down a toilet? What about cutting up the baby for baby parts so the parts can be sold?

The question being asked is: "Will God take this land from us and give it back to the Native American Indians or to another nation"?

There are two main reasons and they really matter to God, so we must be honest and face reality.

Let's look back into history to the year 30 common era as we read what is written in Leviticus 23:15,16 NKJ - **15** 'And you shall count for yourselves from the day after the Sabbath, from the day that you brought the sheaf of the wave offering: seven Sabbaths shall be completed. **16** Count fifty days to the day after the seventh Sabbath; then you shall offer a new grain offering to the LORD.

Leviticus tells us that this is a Holy Day commanded by God, a feast is being described. Do the people of today honor this Holy time set apart to worship God? God has set laws in place to be observed throughout time, this means up to today and into infinity (forever). Hebrews 13:8 NKJ - **8** Jesus Christ *is* the same yesterday, today, and forever. What does this verse mean? Jesus Christ will not and can not change! Does that also mean that Jesus Christ is God? Yes it does! John 1:1 NKJ - **1** In the beginning was the Word, and the Word was with God, and the Word was God. John 10:30 NKJ – (Jesus said), **30 I and *My* Father are one."** (This means they are one God or one Godhead, Elohim in Hebrew, one unit comprised of two parts.)

CHAPTER SIXTEEN
CHRISTIANITY BEGINS

The Apostles and the Jews, the tribe of Judah, were assembled keeping the feast in Acts 2:1 thru 4 NKJ - **1** When the Day of Pentecost had fully come, they were all with one accord in one place. **2** And suddenly there came a sound from heaven, as of a rushing mighty wind, and it filled the whole house where they were sitting. **3** Then there appeared to them divided tongues, as of fire, and *one* sat upon each of them. **4** And they were all filled with the Holy Spirit and began to speak with other tongues, as the Spirit gave them utterance.

In the English language, the Greek word pneuma means wind or breath. Literally the Holy Breath of God came into the Apostles with the sound of a rushing mighty wind and empowered them with miraculous power, this is called receiving the Holy Spirit (NKJ).

The facts are clear and it really matters how the beginning of Christianity began. Jesus Christ Himself began Christianity in a Jewish society approximately 2,000 years ago. The Apostles were Jews by religion observing the true Sabbath which He had ordained and made Holy in the beginning at Creation. The laws of the Sabbath and the Holy Days are mentioned in Leviticus 23. These are God's laws written for us too because we are being told in scripture Hebrews 13:8 NKJ - **8** Jesus Christ *is* the same yesterday, today, and forever. This verse is explaining to us that what we do spiritually today matters! The connection we make today with our Lord Jesus Christ reaches out into the future forever. We also need to understand the Sabbath and the Holy Days just as the Apostles were required to know the truth.

The Apostle Paul was a Benjamite, (from the tribe of Benjamin by blood), a Jew by religion and a Pharisee.

Jesus chose these men for the very reason they were already keeping the Passover, the weekly Sabbath and the Holy Days. Jesus did not have to teach them these Holy days but would have had to if He had selected Gentiles, non-Jews to become His Apostles.

Genesis 2:1 thru 3 NKJ - **1** Thus the heavens and the earth, and all the host of them, were finished. **2** And on the seventh day God ended His work which He had done, and He rested on the seventh day from all His work which He had done. **3** Then God blessed the seventh day and sanctified it, because in it He rested from all His work which God had created and made.

Observing and studying the annual Sabbaths and the Holy Days opens up our minds and reveals the plan of God for all of mankind.

Many people never considered asking themselves, "Why am I here?" "What is God's plan that He has planned from the beginning?" There must be more about life and about His purpose for us than to be born, grow up, propagate, then die; as the animals do.

Most Protestant Churches of today or the Catholic Church neither one observe God's weekly Sabbath or His Holy Days. Neither do they observe the Passover in the prescribed manner. They hold a Eucharist which is a substitute in place of the Passover called Communion or the Lord's Supper. Churches today are no longer the true Ecclesia of Christ and as we see how our young women are slaughtering their babies, how can our nation survive? The things that the churches are doing are made up in the minds of men. Looking today at all the Churches that have fallen away (apostatized) from the way Jesus and the Apostles established His Church, what incentive is there for God to keep blessing us and propping up this nation? The question must be asked, "How much longer under these circumstances can America survive or is America doomed"?

CHAPTER SEVENTEEN

LOVE A SPLENDID THING

We have all heard that 'love is a many splendored' thing and it certainly does take a lot of adjectives to describe all the ways it does affect people.

Biblically speaking there are mainly three categories of love but they branch out to cover many emotions and aspects of human character plus the character of God.

In the New Testament love is used as a verb 'agapaō' and a noun 'agapẽ' in Greek.

Then there is the Greek word phileo expressing "tender affection" or "brotherly love".

1 John 4:8, 16 NKJ - **8** He who does not love does not know God, for God is love. **16** And we have known and believed the love that God has for us. God is love, and he who abides in love abides in God, and God in him.

We can get a sense of the love a husband and father have for his family from biblical examples. Even though Absalom killed his brother Amnon, his father King David still had a fierce love in his grieving heart for Absalom.

2 Samuel 13:28,29,37 thru 39 NKJ - **28** Now Absalom had commanded his servants, saying, "Watch now,

when Amnon's heart is merry with wine, and when I say to you, 'Strike Amnon!' then kill him. Do not be afraid. Have I not commanded you? Be courageous and valiant." **29** So the servants of Absalom did to Amnon as Absalom had commanded. Then all the king's sons arose, and each one got on his mule and fled. **37** But Absalom fled and went to Talmai the son of Ammihud, king of Geshur. And *David* mourned for his son every day. **38** So Absalom fled and went to Geshur, and was there three years. **39** And King David longed to go to Absalom. For he had been comforted concerning Amnon, because he was dead.

Another example of splendid love is the prodigal son who wasted his inheritance but his father gave him a job when he returned home broke and destitute, even giving him a big welcome home party.

The words in scripture tell it best, Luke 15:11 thru 32 NKJ - **11** Then He (Jesus) said: **"A certain man had two sons. 12 And the younger of them said to *his* father, 'Father, give me the portion of goods that falls *to me.*' So he divided to them *his* livelihood. 13 And not many days after, the younger son gathered all together, journeyed to a far country, and there wasted his possessions with prodigal living. 14 But when he had spent all, there arose a severe famine in that land, and he began to be in want. 15 Then he went and joined himself to a citizen of that country, and he sent him into his fields to feed swine. 16 And he would gladly have filled his stomach with the pods that the swine ate, and no one gave him *anything.* 17 But when he came to himself, he said, 'How** many of my father's hired servants have bread enough and to spare, and I perish with hunger! **18** I will arise and go to my father, and will say to him, "Father, I have sinned against heaven and before you, **19** and I am no longer worthy to be called your son. Make me like one of your hired servants." ' **20** And he arose and came to his father. But when he was still a great way off, his father saw him and had compassion, and ran and fell on his neck and kissed him. **21** And the son said to him, 'Father, I have sinned against heaven and in your sight, and am no longer worthy to be called your son.' **22** But the father said to his servants, 'Bring out the best robe and put *it* on him, and put a ring on his hand and sandals on *his* feet. **23** And bring the fatted calf here and kill *it,* and let us eat and be merry; **24** for this my son was dead and is alive again; he was lost and is found.' And they began to be merry. **25** Now his older son was in the field. And as he came and drew near to the house, he heard music and dancing. **26** So he called one of the servants and asked what these things meant. **27** And he said to him, 'Your brother has come, and because he has received him safe and sound, your father has killed the fatted calf.' **28** But he was angry and would not go in. Therefore his father came out and pleaded with him. **29** So he answered and said to *his* father, 'Lo, these many years I have been serving you; I never transgressed your commandment at any time; and yet you never gave me a young goat, that I might make merry with my friends. **30** But as soon as this son of yours came, who has

devoured your livelihood with harlots, you killed the fatted calf for him.' 31 And he said to him, 'Son, you are always with me, and all that I have is yours. 32 It was right that we should make merry and be glad, for your brother was dead and is alive again, and was lost and is found.' "

Don't you know when we return to our Saviour He will open up His arms to us and invite us in to sup with Him? This illustrates how deeply God our Father loves us and how deeply we must love our children and our wives as well.

CHAPTER EIGHTEEN
THE IMPORTANCE OF PROPER FOOD

When God created all the animals: fowl, fish, and creeping creatures, marine life and all, He made some of them to feed off of each other.

Sharks and whales eat big fish, big fish eat smaller fish, smaller fish eat snails, shrimp and plankton, algae etcetera. This is the plan God has for marine life, not all marine life is for human consumption.

It is written twice in the Bible the types of underwater creatures that are safe for man to eat. Leviticus chapter 11:9 thru 12 and Deuteronomy 14:9 and 10.

The anatomy of the creatures labeled as human food is designed to filter out impurities of things they may have consumed which would be harmful to a human if eaten.

God made it easy for us to recognize the safe aquatic ones. Those that are safe to eat are those with <u>fins and scales</u>. Bottom feeders such as in the catfish family have no scales, they are scavengers (bottom feeders). The catfish has a purpose to clean up the bottom of rivers, lakes and ponds and should not be eaten by human beings.

It is not surprising though to realize that there are hundreds of catfish farms across America where people raise catfish for restaurant's in defiance of God's warning.

Many people flock to these catfish eateries like sharks on a feeding frenzy eager to eat what God told them to shun. The human digestive system is not made to properly assimilate the type of flesh on these fish, those with no fins and scales.

God has commanded us to avoid such things but like a defiant child we have become gluttons after what we should not have.

The human anatomy is surely wonderfully made and it surely takes a lot of abuse from the food that we eat.

Half of the healthcare facilities in the USA would more than likely be put out of business if people were to obey God regarding their diet.

God tells us to eat the right things and eat in moderation; this is very important and this really matters! If we were to obey God in our eating habits, to realize and accept the facts as God has intended for us to do we would have a much better day in how we feel, how we act and how we think.

As we have mentioned in a previous chapter there is a lot that is against our health, chemicals and poisons used are already in the environment and what has been done to our food has become a normal practice.

IMPORTANT THINGS THAT REALLY MATTER

The farmers on a farm or a ranch want to sell their produce at a higher rate. Greed by the growers have caused them to push animals beyond the range of sensibility to put more weight, more pounds on them faster, to sell them for more money. This is beyond normal, beyond being sensible.

The cattle are fed more food plus they are fed grain laced with steroids to make them fatter which makes them tender on the plate just before taking them to market.

Notice what God said He created for us to eat in the animal kingdom taken from Leviticus 11:1 thru 8 NKJ - **1** Now the LORD spoke to Moses and Aaron, saying to them, **2** "Speak to the children of Israel, saying, 'These *are* the animals which you may eat among all the animals that *are* on the earth: **3** Among the animals, whatever divides the hoof, having cloven hooves *and* chewing the cud--that you may eat. **4** Nevertheless these you shall not eat among those that chew the cud or those that have cloven hooves: the camel, because it chews the cud but does not have cloven hooves, is unclean to you; **5** the rock hyrax, because it chews the cud but does not have cloven hooves, *is* unclean to you; **6** the hare, because it chews the cud but does not have cloven hooves, *is* unclean to you; **7** and the swine, though it divides the hoof, having cloven hooves, yet does not chew the cud, *is* unclean to you. **8** Their flesh you shall not eat, and their carcasses you shall not touch. They *are* unclean to you.

These laws were given to us to prevent disease and enable longevity of life. Animals like cow, sheep and goats have multiple stomachs which filter out most harmful elements in what they eat before it is assimilated in to their flesh, so they are a clean animal for humans to eat.

The same information is given concerning these animals in Deuteronomy 14:1 thru 8 NKJ - **1** "You *are* the children of the LORD your God; you shall not cut yourselves nor shave the front of your head for the dead. **2** For you *are* a holy people to the LORD your God, and the LORD has chosen you to be a people for Himself, a special treasure above all the peoples who *are* on the face of the earth. **3** "You shall not eat any detestable thing. **4** These *are* the animals which you may eat: the ox, the sheep, the goat, **5** the deer, the gazelle, the roe deer, the wild goat, the mountain goat, the antelope, and the mountain sheep. **6** And you may eat every animal with cloven hooves, having the hoof split into two parts, *and that* chews the cud, among the animals. **7** Nevertheless, of those that chew the cud or have cloven hooves, you shall not eat, *such as* these: the camel, the hare, and the rock hyrax; for they chew the cud but do not have cloven hooves; they *are* unclean for you. **8** Also the swine is unclean for you, because it has cloven hooves, yet *does* not *chew* the cud; you shall not eat their flesh or touch their dead carcasses.

God gave us basic health laws to ward off disease but people often ask if it is a sin to eat these animals? What is sin? Sin is missing the mark by disobeying

God! What is our attitude as we stuff our jaw with crabmeat or catfish or ham from a swine?

We have to realize that we forfeit our God given protection from disease when we deliberately defy God and eat those things He warned us not to eat. Many people do eat the wrong things for many years with no significant evidence of illness because of their diet; but they are the lucky ones; thousands have died miserably agonizing deaths from rabbit fever, tularemia from squirrels and rabbits and trichinosis from pork.

Romans 6:23 NKJ - **23** For the wages of sin *is* death, but the gift of God *is* eternal life in Christ Jesus our Lord.

Death from either of these rodent born diseases are extremely painful. It is indeed very sad and shameful that people will not listen and obey the wisdom of He who created us and told us what to avoid.

Adam and Eve did not obey either they ate the forbidden fruit and look what that caused. It is so much better to say "God said it and I believe it, as for me and my house we will serve the Lord"!

We will get into more than enough harmful things accidently without defying the clear instructions of God. Most of us who grew up eating ground hogs, raccoons, squirrels, rabbits and swine do not realize how lucky we are to be alive and feeling well.

A disease resulting from infestation with Trichinella spiralis occurs in humans caused by ingestion of infested pork. The symptoms are fever, muscle weakness and diarrhea accompanied with much pain.

Years ago in the ghettos of the large American cities people died by the hundreds and no one knew what was killing them until they noticed that none of those who had died were Jews. The answer is a simple one, Jews do not eat pork.

The Jewish ghettos were untouched by this disease so a very intense investigation was launched by the health department.

The only major difference they could find in the diet of what was being sold at the grocery store in all of these neighborhoods was that the Jews did not buy pork. This was when and how the trichina worm was discovered and the source from which it came.

The eggs hatch out in the stomach and intestines of an infected person and bore their way through the lining into the surrounding muscle tissue.

The infection tears into the muscle tissue like termites tear into wood. This causes a very slow and painful death from a disease known as trichinosis.

Around 1920 to 1925 in Tulare County, California was the time rabbit fever was diagnosed and documented. People were coming down with intermittent fever and swelling of lymph nodes and severe muscle pain.

Mainly this is a disease of rodents and can be transmitted to human beings who eat rabbit and/or squirrel. This disease is also transmitted by deer flies drawing blood from rabbits or squirrels then biting humans or other animals.

Any insect such as a tick who has access to an infected rodent can transmit this disease to humans too.

Eating squirrels or rabbits can be very risky and can be very deadly.

God gave us animals to eat and they have the description of a divided hoof and chew the cud, like a cow. To eat any other kind is to put yourself at great risk of horrendous illness and possibly death.

Raccoons are the most common culprit in carrying a disease called rabies. This disease ends with death to most of its victims, yet some people still eat raccoons.

Rabies is usually transmitted by a bite from an infected animal. It is common for dogs, cats, human beings or nearly any animal to be bitten by a rabid animal.

A rabid animal is violently intense, furious, and mad; they walk like a staggering drunk, they are fearless. They will attack anything or anyone that comes near them.

Every parent has a responsibility to protect their children as best as they can from these diseases and avoid eating these types of animals. We need to learn from what Adam did as he and Eve ate the forbidden fruit.

It is interesting to notice how people today use the same argument Eve did as she was being tempted to eat the forbidden fruit in Genesis 3:6 NKJ - **6** So when the woman saw that the tree *was* <u>good for food</u>, that it *was* <u>pleasant to the eyes</u>, and a tree desirable to make *one* wise, she took of its fruit and ate. She also gave to her husband with her, and he ate.

Today we look at a sugar cured ham in the same way Eve looked at the forbidden fruit. It is the same scenario! God said for them not to eat it but it looked enticing and the end result was death.

Death is the penalty for sin and sin is disobedience to God and the law is the same for our protection.

Leviticus 11:7, Deuteronomy 14:8, Isaiah 65:1 thru 5, and Isaiah 66:3,17 should be read and marked in your Bible.

Some folks argue that this is an Old Testament teaching and that it does not apply to Christians of the New Testament church era.

When did God change the anatomy of hogs or when did He change the anatomy of humans? Hogs are still hogs and humans are still humans and people die just as dead now as they did in the Old Testament days; and they also get just as sick.

Our food processing centers have gone to great lengths to figure out ways to make naturally unsafe animals safe to eat but pork is still the main culprit in hardening of the arteries in aging people, but not the only cause.

Read the ingredients on many items on the shelf at your local grocery store and you will find that pork is processed in almost all products. It is not wise to buy these products! They look good, they taste good and they can make you sick.

During the depression years of the 1930's many poor people survived eating these unclean animals but today times are not that hard and there is no excuse for modern day people to have to eat something as risky to their health as these vermin, rodents or swine.

Naturally people want to be blessed, but the problem is that most seem to want blessings and freedom without giving any regard to God. A big problem is that most people do not know what God wants, nor do they care! They want good health without regard to diet.

Sin, which is disobedience to God, closes the door to being blessed and opens the door to receive curses, correction and judgments or penalties.

This is true in every facet of our lives, health included. It has been this way with Israel down through the years from ancient times to modern times as was warned in Deuteronomy 28:1 thru 14 which are known as the blessings for the obedient and the remainder of the chapter tells of the curses for not obeying God.

We know the Jews have a belief as do a lot of Christians that God's plan covers a span of 6,000 years for mankind to govern himself on the earth. 2 Peter 3:8 NKJ - **8** But, beloved, do not forget this one thing, that with the Lord one day *is* as a thousand years, and a thousand years as one day.

If this is true we are nearing the completion of the six thousand years. According to the Comprehensive Hebrew Calendar by Arthur Spier we are now in the year 5776 from creation. This means there are 224 more years until Jesus Christ assumes Kingship over the earth and ushers in the millennium.

That will mark the end of men ruling over men in every country on the earth. Many positions will be delegated by Jesus Christ to the resurrected saints not humans.

Scripturally it seems to stack up this way. Jesus Christ will be King over all the earth during the millennium, King David will be resurrected and be king over a new Israel, and the twelve Apostles will sit on thrones judging the twelve tribes of new Israel during the millennium.

There will be one thousand years of doing things God's way with no exceptions which has never been done since man was put on the earth.

God did not limit the number of years a man or woman could live in the first century, Common Era, but He did apparently set a day in His view to be one thousand years in man's view. God has never yet allowed a man or women to live a full millennial day, (1,000 years). Methuselah, the grandfather of Noah, came the closest by living 969 years. Noah was second he lived 960 years.

Later God set a limit of 120 years for man to live, which was later shortened again to just 70 years. Living longer allowed evil men to spread their wickedness farther and to more of the younger people as populations continued to spread. By cutting their longevity back God was able to curtail some of the spread of evil and slow it down.

As previously mentioned in Genesis 6:5 wickedness had spread, and became so bad, that God killed everyone but Noah and his family of eight people.

There is something about this that needs to be brought to our attention. Everyone seems to know the story of Noah and the Ark and how the animals came to him and he loaded them on the ark.

Obviously these were baby animals just weaned from their mothers and were brought to the ark by angels not visible to the human eye.

The important thing to notice here is how many of each kind of these animals there were.

Genesis 7:2 thru 6, 24 NKJ - **2** You shall take with you seven each of every clean animal, a male and his female; two each of animals that *are* unclean, a male and his female; **3** also seven each of birds of the air, male and female, to keep the species alive on the face of all the earth. **4** For after seven more days I will cause it to rain on the earth forty days and forty nights, and I will destroy from the face of the earth all living things that I have made." **5** And Noah did according to all that the LORD commanded him. **6** Noah *was* six hundred years old when the floodwaters were on the earth. **24** And the waters prevailed on the earth one hundred and fifty days.

Next comes another very important thing that needs to be noticed in Genesis 8:20 NKJ - **20** Then Noah built an altar to the LORD, and took of every clean animal and of every clean bird, and offered burnt offerings on the altar.

This is why Noah was instructed to take seven of the clean animals and birds. They would propagate faster and in more abundance because they were needed for sacrifices and for food. The others did not matter so much, they were here for other reasons not for food or sacrifices.

God also designated certain birds to be for human food and others were not to be eaten. Both the animals and fowl that were for food had multiple stomachs and/or chewed the cud whereas the others did not.

Birds that are hawks or vultures in type do not have a gizzard and should not be eaten by people. Birds like chickens, guines, turkeys, ducks, geese etc. have a crop (stomach) and a gizzard so what they eat gets filtered before it is assimilated into their flesh. In the insect family grasshoppers may be eaten but not many Americans bother dining on them. Leviticus 11:47 NKJ - [47] to distinguish between the unclean and the clean, and between the animal that may be eaten and the animal that may not be eaten.

CHAPTER NINETEEN
THE POWER OF POSITIVE READING

Today when we turn on the radio or the television especially on Sunday our eyes and ears are treated with, in some cases, a very audacious clergy. Some can be quite brazen in their claims of what is necessary to attain salvation, and it usually involves them receiving money, lots of money.

In other cases it may be what one news commentator terms as bloviating blatherskites. One minister recently meekly and humbly asked the public for only one million dollars that was desperately needed "right away".

A few years ago a "faith healer" was asking for two million dollars to help him build a hospital; why would a faith healer need a hospital? A Texas oil man bailed him out because the public was not quite that gullible yet, then his benefactor advised him to go get some "professional help".

It is hard to say this, and hard to realize and accept, how much fraud there is in religion. Religion today is a set of philosophies built by opinions of men.

It is imperative to emphasize that there is power in positive reading. To do this one has to take the Bible literally and put doctrines of all corporate church organizations in the back seat of our mind.

The clear question here is, do we want to establish a relationship with Jesus Christ, our Saviour, or with a church corporation?

The clear message of the Bible is always positive it is not about failure it is about overcoming evil with good! The Bible is not about fear, yet hundreds of preachers always preach a fear tactic religion. They exclaim to the top of their lungs that there is a heaven to gain and a hell to shun. That distorted message did not come from the Bible! All one has to do is believe Jesus Christ when He said what He did in John 3:13 NKJ - **13 No one has ascended to heaven but He who came down from heaven,** *that is,* **the Son of Man who is in heaven.**

The clear reader will see that ever since Lucifer was banished and exiled from heaven he has wanted to get back there, without repenting of course.

Satan has deceived most church goers of today into believing heaven will be their eternal reward, but Jesus said just the opposite!

The Apostle Paul termed Satan the god of this world, 2 Corinthians 4:3,4 NKJ – **3** But even if our gospel is veiled, it is veiled to those who are perishing, **4** whose minds the god of this age has blinded, who do not believe, lest the light of the gospel of the glory of Christ, who is the image of God, should shine on them.

We have two accounts of the fall of Satan; Isaiah 14:12 thru 15 and Ezekiel 28:12 thru 19, Satan is promised the same fate as the king of Tyre whom he had influenced to ruin. It is clear that eventually Satan will be destroyed by something like a spiritual bolt of lightning because a physical fire would have no effect on a spirit being.

Bringing all of this to light is obviously going to raise the question in the minds of our readers, just what is salvation, and how is it given to humans, and where do they go to receive it? This is big!

It would be wise to understand a very important principle given in Isaiah 28:9,10,13 NKJ - **9** "Whom will he teach knowledge? And whom will he make to understand the message? Those *just* weaned from milk? Those *just* drawn from the breasts? **10** For precept *must be* upon precept, precept upon precept, line upon line, line upon line, here a little, there a little."   **13** But the word of the LORD was to them, "Precept upon precept, precept upon precept, line upon line, line upon line, here a little, there a little," That they might go and fall backward, and be broken and snared and caught.

It takes a lot of reading to familiarize one's self with the Bible.

After reading the Bible through several times the little pieces begin to come together and the big picture begins to take shape. It truly is line upon line, here a little and there a little.

In a similar fashion evil spread in the first millennium (1,000 years), from Adam largely, and partly due to people living a long time, now we have ways of preserving and storing truth that can be preserved for the indefinite future, perhaps if necessary up to thousands of years if that becomes necessary.

We must know that we are born with a human nature, which means we are born with an enmity to God. Romans 8:7 NKJ - **7** Because the carnal mind *is* enmity against God; for it is not subject to the law of God, nor indeed can be. And James 4:4 NKJ - Do you not know that friendship with the world is enmity with God?

Casual reading may be beneficial if one is reading for entertainment and just to pass the time, but when reading for instructions of righteous living and for healthy living, it is imperative that we be in a positive frame of mind, even a prayerful frame of mind.

Paying attention to details like time lines and specific events will build a reservoir of knowledge into our psyche where it is stored ready for instant recall whenever and wherever it may be needed.

There is power in knowledge, this is why the educated elderly are the people sought out when sage advice and wisdom are needed. This was one of the main functions of church elders in the first century Common Era.

A church elder was not a position, not a rank, but a service of "overseer". By their conduct and service they had shown spiritual conduct and maturity and they took care of the needs of their congregation such as praying for and anointing the sick, seeing to the needs of the widows and orphans and serving as spiritual advisors to the deacons which was a physical service. Acts 6:1 thru 4 NKJ - **1** Now in those days, when *the number of* the disciples was multiplying, there arose a complaint against the Hebrews by the Hellenists, because their widows were neglected in the daily distribution. **2** Then the twelve summoned the multitude of the disciples and said, "It is not desirable that we should leave the word of God and serve tables. **3** Therefore, brethren, seek out from among you seven men of *good* reputation, full of the Holy Spirit and wisdom, whom we may appoint over this business; **4** but we will give ourselves continually to prayer and to the ministry of the word."

We learn as we journey through life that many, many things are important and really matter. In every aspect of life that we are confronted with we can see that the most important things that really matter are not the secular things but the spiritual things.

Unfortunately the spiritual things are ignored more than the physical and the secular. We need to call attention to some of the spiritual because whether we might want to realize and accept it or not, all of us are ultimately going to meet our maker.

This is why we want to stress the power of positive reading. Push opinions, doctrines, and philosophies of men to the side and zero in on what God is saying to us individually in His Word. After all the Bible is dubbed the instruction book to life.

We are not only interested in our lives now but we are interested in the truth of what lies beyond. There are a lot of opinions of men that are helpful and wise but all of them should be weighed against what we find in the Word of God.

Let's give pause now to some of the areas that need attention concerning the power of positive reading. Genesis 2:1 thru 3 NKJ - **1** Thus the heavens and the earth, and all the host of them, were finished. **2** And on the seventh day God ended His work which He had done, and He rested on the seventh day from all His work which He had done. **3** Then God blessed the seventh day and sanctified it, because in it He rested from all His work which God had created and made.

Even though people know Emperor Constantine 1 of Rome passed a secular civil law, in 312 C.E., that all religions in the Roman Empire would be required to worship on Sunday. After the Protestant Reformation they did not return to the Sabbath worship. Most Protestants continue to worship on the first day of the week, with few exceptions, to this very day, in defiance of the 4th commandment, Deuteronomy 5:12 thru 15.

The exceptions are the 7th Day Baptists, 7th Day Adventists and the Church of God 7th Day and many scattered Church of God independent groups.

People have grown accustomed to reading scriptures pertaining to the Sabbath glossing over in their minds that it is the seventh day and affixing the first day in its place until it is a permanent psychological implant.

That does not change the scriptures and it does not change the facts and it holds the reader prisoner to error. The power to freedom is accept the plain truth and that can only be done by accepting truth from the Bible.

Another area that needs attention is the question often asked, "Is eternity in heaven the reward of the saved?" The short answer is written in John 3:13 NKJ - **13 No one has ascended to heaven but He who came down from heaven, *that is,* the Son of Man who is in heaven.**

In conjunction with that, it is not widely taught, therefore not understood, what eternity or being eternal means. Eternal is always existing without a beginning, now present, and without an end.

Every human being has had a beginning so we do not fit the definition. Resurrected Christians will be given immortality and can never die again, but they had a beginning. Jesus Christ and the Father had no beginning, they are presently existing and always will exist, they are eternal spirit beings something no human can ever metamorph into.

We can enter spirit life from a certain point on through infinity but that is not eternal because we have a starting point. In his letters the Apostle Paul always refers to immortality but never eternal life.

Certain churches in recent years have invented a new term for the resurrection, they call it the rapture when in actuality rapture is an emotion; it is not an event.

Many bewildered people ask, "Where do the resurrected saints go because Jesus said they are not going to heaven?" It is written in I Thessalonians 4:17 that both the living who are changed into spirit beings at Christs coming for the saints and those who are resurrected will be caught up together to meet Christ in the air but it does not say they are taken to heaven.

CHAPTER TWENTY
WHAT IS HEAVEN

We have established that heaven is not the reward of the saved; as a matter of fact there are actually three areas referred to as heaven in the Holy Bible.

The <u>first heaven</u> is the Earth's atmosphere where the wind and gentle breezes blow and where rain and snow fall from the clouds and touch the ground.

Psalms 147:7,8 NKJ - **7** Sing to the LORD with thanksgiving; sing praises on the harp to our God, **8** Who covers the heavens with clouds, Who prepares rain for the earth, Who makes grass to grow on the mountains.

Job 35:5 NKJ - **5** Look to the heavens and see; and behold the clouds--they are higher than you.

Jeremiah 34:20 NKJ - **20** I will give them into the hand of their enemies and into the hand of those who seek their life. Their dead bodies shall be for meat for the birds of the heaven and the beasts of the earth.

The <u>second</u> area referred to as heaven is above the earth's atmosphere where the stars and planets decorate the sky in the darkness of the night.

Psalms 8:3 NKJ - **3** When I consider Your heavens, the work of Your fingers, the moon and the stars, which You have ordained.

Genesis 26:4 NKJ - **4** And I will make your descendants multiply as the stars of heaven; I will give to your descendants all these lands; and in your seed all the nations of the earth shall be blessed.

Isaiah 13:10 NKJ - **10** For the stars of heaven and their constellations will not give their light; the sun will be darkened in its going forth, and the moon will not cause its light to shine.

The <u>third</u> area referred to as heaven in the Bible is the spiritual realm known as the place where God and the angels and all the heavenly creatures abide. This is where Lucifer was banished, exiled from when he rebelled and became Satan.

Isaiah 14:12 thru 17 NKJ - **12** "How you are fallen from heaven, O Lucifer, son of the morning! *How* you are cut down to the ground, you who weakened the nations! **13** For you have said in your heart: 'I will ascend into heaven, I will exalt my throne above the stars of God; I will also sit on the mount of the congregation on the farthest sides of the north; **14** I will ascend above the heights of the clouds, I will be like the Most High.' **15** Yet you shall be brought down to Sheol (hell), to the lowest depths of the Pit. **16** "Those who see you will gaze at you, *and* consider you, *saying:* '*Is* this the man who made the earth tremble, who shook kingdoms, **17** Who made the world as a wilderness and destroyed its cities, *who* did not open the house of his prisoners?'

Satan has longed to return to his former abode but cannot, read verse 13 again. His retaliation from being banished from the third heaven is to deceive the Christian world into believing they are going to go to the third heaven when they depart this physical life.

Apostle Paul wrote in 2 Corinthians 12:2 thru 4 NKJ - **2** I know a man in Christ who fourteen years ago--whether in the body I do not know, or whether out of the body I do not know, God knows--such a one was caught up to the third heaven. **3** And I know such a man--whether in the body or out of the body I do not know, God knows-- **4** how he was caught up into Paradise and heard inexpressible words, which it is not lawful for a man to utter.

There are other scriptures that mention this third heaven. 1 Kings 8:49 NKJ - **49** then hear in heaven Your (God's) dwelling place their prayer and their supplication, and maintain their cause.

2 Chronicles 6:30, 39 NKJ - **30** then hear from heaven Your (God's) dwelling place, and forgive, and give to everyone according to all his ways, whose heart You know (for You alone know the hearts of the sons of men). **39** then hear from heaven Your (God's) dwelling place their prayer and their supplications, and maintain their cause, and forgive Your people who have sinned against You.

Revelation 19:14 NKJ - **14** And the armies (angels) in heaven, clothed in fine linen, white and clean, followed Him on white horses.

Revelation 14:17 NKJ - **17** Then another angel came out of the temple which is in heaven, he also having a sharp sickle.

Thousands upon thousands of well-meaning sincere people are believing they are "heaven bound" when there is not one verse of scripture that tells us heaven is the reward of the saved.

God has something totally different in His mind, whether one is resurrected in the 1st resurrection or resurrected in the 2nd resurrection. God ultimately will change them to immortal beings according to His plan.

The capstone verse in this discussion is in John 3:13 NKJ - **13** No one has ascended to heaven but He who came down from heaven, *that is,* the Son of Man who is in heaven.

Many church folks believe in the immortal soul, believing the soul stands alone and that it goes to heaven, hell or purgatory when the body goes to the grave.

The truth of this matter is this belief never came from the Bible. When God breathed into Adam's nostrils, Adam became a living soul, he was not given a living soul, he was a living soul.

In the Old Testament the Hebrew word, "nephesh" is rendered "soul" in the King James Version of the Bible. Nephesh is defined as a living creature drawing breath. It applies to animals, fowl and humans. To use the King James English all of these creatures are a living soul.

To make a statement such as: "A soul is in hell", is the same as saying you buried a living person, for a soul is a living breathing creature.

What does "Eternal life" mean? A standard dictionary says the word means: "Without beginning", "Now present" and "Without end". Every human being has had a starting point or a beginning and even if they are granted "everlasting life" they still had a beginning, so people do not fit the mold of eternal life. However there is life lasting into the unending future which means "Everlasting Life". The Apostle Paul called everlasting life immortality which is more accurate.

Only the Heavenly Father and Jesus Christ fit the description "Eternal Life". Revelation 22:13 NKJ – (Jesus said), **13 I am the Alpha and the Omega, *the* Beginning and *the* End, the First and the Last."** Hebrews 7:3 NKJ - **3** without father, without mother, without genealogy, having neither beginning of days nor end of life, but made like the Son of God, remains a priest continually. Genesis 14:18 NKJ – **18** Then Melchizedek king of Salem brought out bread and wine; he *was* the priest of God Most High.

There is an order of the priesthood in the third heaven called the order of Melchizdek Priesthood and He serves as priest to the Most High God, the Father written in the Old Testament.

In the New Testament, Hebrews 5:6 NKJ - **6** As *He also says* in another *place: "You are a priest forever according to the order of Melchizedek".*

Hebrews 7:1 thru 3 NKJ - **1** For this Melchizedek, king of Salem, priest of the Most High God, who met Abraham returning from the slaughter of the kings and blessed him, **2** to whom also Abraham gave a tenth part of all, first being translated "king of righteousness," and then also king of Salem, meaning "king of peace," **3** without father, without mother, without genealogy, having neither beginning of days nor end of life, but made like the Son of God, remains a priest continually.

Psalms 110:4 NKJ - **4** The Lord has sworn and will not relent, "You *are* a priest forever according to the order of Melchizedek."

It is fairly obvious that Jesus Christ who is also prophet, priest and king is this Melchizedek.

When the land of Israel became established in 1405 B,C., the Levitical priesthood was installed in the tabernacle (tent) at first and the temple was built in Solomon's day. The Levites had charge of all the duties and the priests were in courses which means they took turns serving in the temple according to the order of the Levitical Priesthood patterned after the

Melchizedek Priesthood. All priests were Levities, from the tribe of Levi descendants of Aaron.

WHAT HAPPENS WHEN WE DIE

The erroneous concept is that the soul departs the body and the soul either goes to heaven or hell or purgatory. This is a superstition and a false belief; these ideas never came from the Bible.

The Bible tells us a living breathing human being is a soul. When a person expires their last breath goes out of the lungs and that person's spirit goes out of the body with the last breath; they go out at the same time, together. The breath mingles with the air and their spirit goes back to God who gave it.

There is a spirit in mankind but it is not a soul. In Greek the spirit is pneuma the same word as wind or breath so the spirit is in the breath and when the last breath goes out the spirit goes with it. Ecclesiastes 12:7 NKJ - **7** Then the dust will return to the earth as it was, and the spirit will return to God who gave it.

The Old Testament word 'spirit' is from the Hebrew word "ruah" with means breath, air, strength, wind, breeze, spirit, courage, temper.

Acts 2:2 NKJ - **2** And suddenly there came a sound from heaven, as of a rushing mighty wind, and it filled the whole house where they were sitting. This verse is a good example of spirit called wind. In this case when the "Holy Pneuma" was given to the church it came in as a sound of rushing mighty wind. Spirit essence is not a spirit being, it is a force and energy, a disembodied element in people giving us energy, character and personality.

We have energy, character and personality on a natural level, then when we are given God's Holy Spirit it is on a higher spirit level enabling us to walk as Jesus Christ walked and to imitate Him in our life style. This higher spirit level is given to the saints at the first resurrection. The saints are resurrected with a new spirit body such as the angels have, but the human spirit has gone back to God, Ecclesiastes 12:7. God will give back your spirit elevated to a higher spirit level and will unite that spirit with a new spirit body.

The first ones to be resurrected will have been judged worthy, at the same time they will receive a spirit body and their Holy Spirit (one that is not human). These resurrected saints will be taken to the sea of glass.

THE FALSE TRINITY

There are some things that are really important that should be mentioned; the Bible does not teach a trinity! The trinity is an invention of the Roman Catholic Church from the fourth century and was carried over into Protestantism after the Protestant Reformation was over and it still lingers with Protestant churches today. It seems no amount of reasoning can dislodge this false belief.

The Roman Catholic Church gave personhood to a spirit, the Holy Spirit that has no body, spiritual or otherwise and when it was printed in the Old King James Bible they called it the Holy Ghost. A ghost is perceived to be a disembodied spirit in a superstitious set of beliefs.

The Bible teaches only the Father and the Son who are called the Elohim in Hebrew of the Old Testament; there is no third party in the Godhead!

CHAPTER TWENTY ONE
THE REWARD OF THE SAVED

Heaven is never mentioned as being the reward of the saved so the question remains, "Where will the resurrected saints and other saints spend eternity?

As we read earlier in John 3:13 it explains Jesus Christ is the only one who has or will come into heaven after being resurrected. All others will be escorted to the "sea of glass" which is stretched out over the Middle-East from Mt. Sinai to Jerusalem to the River Chebar at a place we call today the country of Iraq.

Jesus is coming back again to gather His saints and He with His angels will escort them to the sea of glass to make preparation for the marriage banquet and the wedding of the spiritual bride of Christ, consisting of 144,000 resurrected saints. (Revelation 19:7 thru 9).

To put this together correctly we need to begin with 1 Thessalonians 4:13 thru 17 NKJ - **13** But I do not want you to be ignorant, brethren, concerning those who have fallen asleep, lest you sorrow as others who have no hope. **14** For if we believe that Jesus died and rose again, even so God will bring with Him those who sleep in Jesus. **15** For this we say to you by the word of the Lord, that we who are alive *and* remain until the coming of the Lord will by no means precede those who are asleep. **16** For the Lord Himself will descend from heaven with a shout, with the voice of an archangel, and with the trumpet of God. And the dead in Christ will rise first. **17** Then we who are alive *and* remain shall be caught up together with them in the clouds to meet the Lord in the air. And thus we shall always be with the Lord.

In verse 17, it tells us "And thus we shall always be with the Lord". Notice carefully in Revelation 4:6 NKJ - **6** Before the throne *there was* a sea of glass, like crystal. His throne is on the sea of glass in the first heaven over Mt. Sinai and Jerusalem as it is written in Revelation 4:2 NKJ - **2** Immediately I was in the Spirit; and behold, a throne set in heaven, and *One* sat on the throne. The spiritual world is invisible to the human eye and to any human instrument; but it is in this earth's atmosphere.

Revelation 15:2 NKJ - **2** And I saw *something* like a sea of glass mingled with fire, and those who have the victory over the beast, over his image and over his mark *and* over the number of his name, standing on the sea of glass, having harps of God.

We read in Revelation 14:1 thru 5 that 144,000 are rewarded as being the bride of Christ. Revelation 14:1 thru 5 NKJ - **1** Then I looked, and behold, a Lamb standing on Mount Zion, and with Him <u>one hundred and forty-four thousand</u>, having His Father's name written on their foreheads. **2** And I heard a voice from heaven, like the voice of many waters, and like the voice of loud thunder. And I heard the sound of harpists playing their harps. **3** They sang as it were a new song before the throne, before the four living creatures, and the elders; and no one could learn that song except the hundred *and* forty-four thousand who were redeemed from the earth. **4** These are the ones who were not defiled with women, for they are virgins. These are the ones who follow the Lamb wherever He goes. These were redeemed from *among* men, *being* firstfruits to God and to the Lamb. **5** And in their mouth was found no deceit, for they are without fault before the throne of God. This group of 144,000 is not to be confused with the 144,000 of Revelation 7:3 thru 8.

Revelation 19:7 thru 10 NKJ - **7** Let us be glad and rejoice and give Him glory, for the marriage of the Lamb has come, and His wife has made herself ready." **8** And to her it was granted to be arrayed in fine linen, clean and bright, for the fine linen is the righteous acts of the saints. **9** Then he said to me, "Write: 'Blessed *are* those who are called to the marriage supper of the Lamb!' " And he said to me, "These are the true sayings of God." **10** And I fell at his feet to worship him. But he said to me, "See *that you do* not *do that!* I am your fellow servant, and of your brethren who have the testimony of Jesus. Worship God! For the testimony of Jesus is the spirit of prophecy."

Jesus gives His bride His Father's name as every groom does. These resurrected saints are redeemed from the earth, they are not defiled with false religions, they follow the Lamb (Christ, the groom) wherever He goes as a bride would do and they are the firstfruits of the resurrection to immortality and no guile is spoken by them. Scripture is showing us that the reward of these 144,000, is becoming the bride of Christ.

The other 144,000 of Revelation 7 have a different job and a different assignment to do. This group of 144,000 is made up of physical human beings, they are not resurrected saints. They are the remnant of the original 12 tribes of Israel and they are going to build and grow a new physical Israel during the millennium. They will be sealed for safety and deliverance at a remote location here on the earth, possibly at Petra in the Country of Jordan. They are not on the 'Sea of Glass' and indications are they will not attend the marriage of Christ and His bride which are the resurrected 144,000 saints.

Exodus 19:6 NKJ - **6** And you shall be to Me a kingdom of priests and a holy nation.' These *are* the words which you shall speak to the children of Israel."

This is what ancient Israel was commissioned to do but they failed. The new physical Israel to be raised up during the millennium will not fail, they will start with 144,000 and Christ has a bride of 144,000 spirit beings to aid and assist them!

Isaiah 30:20,21 NKJ - **20** And *though* the Lord gives you the bread of adversity and the water of affliction, yet your teachers will not be moved into a corner anymore, but your eyes shall see your teachers. **21** Your ears shall hear a word behind you, saying, "This *is* the way, walk in it," Whenever you turn to the right hand or whenever you turn to the left.

Not only that but there is an innumerable multitude of resurrected saints that come out of the Great Tribulation who will have positions assigned to them.

Revelation 7:9,10 NKJ - **9** After these things I looked, and behold, a great multitude which no one could number, of all nations, tribes, peoples, and tongues, standing before the throne and before the Lamb, clothed with white robes, with palm branches in their hands, **10** and crying out with a loud voice, saying, "Salvation *belongs* to our God who sits on the throne, and to the Lamb!"

This is a plan of sanctification designed by God that cannot fail and it will not fail. Ultimately it is God's plan to have every human being who has ever lived, those who are living now and those who will live in the future admitted into His spiritual family as His children.

Hebrews 9:27 NKJ - **27** And as it is appointed for men to die once, but after this the judgment.

It is necessary that we lay down this body of flesh. Every human being has to die a physical death once. The only exception will be those who are changed to immortal when Christ returns for the saints.

So we find that the first chapter of the lives of post resurrection saints is to assist in growing the new Israel during the millennium and teach them to live righteous lives.

Even during the millennium every knee will bow and every tongue will confess Jesus Christ is Lord.

John 14:6 NKJ - **6 Jesus said to him, "I am the way, the truth, and the life. No one comes to the Father except through Me.**

Romans 14:11 NKJ - **11** For it is written: *"As I live, says the LORD, Every knee shall bow to Me, And every tongue shall confess to God.*

Philippians 2:10 NKJ - **10** that at the name of Jesus every knee should bow, of those in heaven, and of those on earth, and of those under the earth (these are not yet resurrected).

The truth of the matter is that premillennial saints are required to die once, with one exception 1 Thessalonians 4:17 NKJ - **17** Then we who are alive *and* remain shall be caught up together with them in the clouds to meet the Lord in the air. And thus we shall always be with the Lord.

1 Corinthians 15:51 thru 54 NKJ - **51** Behold, I tell you a mystery: We shall not all sleep, but we shall all be changed-- **52** in a moment, in the twinkling of an eye, at the last trumpet. For the trumpet will sound, and the dead will be raised incorruptible, and we shall be changed. **53** For this corruptible must put on incorruption, and this mortal *must* put on immortality. **54** So when this corruptible has put on incorruption, and this mortal has put on immortality, then shall be brought to pass the saying that is written: *"Death is swallowed up in victory."*

CHAPTER TWENTY TWO
MILLENNIUM TEMPLE

Ezekiel 47:1,11,12 NKJ - **1** Then he brought me back to the door of the temple; and there was water, flowing from under the threshold of the temple toward the east, for the front of the temple faced east; the water was flowing from under the right side of the temple, south of the altar. **11** But its swamps and marshes will not be healed; they will be given over to salt. **12** Along the bank of the river, on this side and that, will grow all *kinds of* trees used for food; their leaves will not wither, and their fruit will not fail. They will bear fruit every month, because their water flows from the sanctuary. Their fruit will be for food, and their leaves for medicine."

When there is no death, people have stopped dying and there ceases to be a necessity for graves.

Revelation 20:14 NKJ - **14** Then Death and Hades (the grave) were cast into the lake of fire. This is the second death.

The end of physical death and the end of graves is called the second death in the Bible. People do not die twice; they live twice! Those who die unconverted face a return to the flesh where they will live for an unspecified amount of time as they are being judged, this is their period of judgment. These people will live until they are judged worthy of immortality then they will be changed to spirit.

Daniel 12:2 NKJ - **2** And many of those who sleep in the dust of the earth shall awake, some to everlasting life, some to shame *and* everlasting contempt (judgment).

Acts 24:15 NKJ - **15** I have hope in God, which they themselves also accept, that there will be a resurrection of *the* dead, both of *the* just and *the* unjust (to a period of judgment).

1 Timothy 2:4 NKJ - **4** who desires all men to be saved and to come to the knowledge of the truth (this is the purpose of the second resurrection).

Revelation 20:13, 14 NKJ - **13** The sea gave up the dead who were in it, and Death and Hades delivered up the dead who were in them. And they were judged, each one according to his works. **14** Then Death and Hades were cast into the lake of fire (a synonym for final judgment). This is the second death.

When those in the second resurrection are finally judged worthy to receive immortality they will be changed to immortal just as the living are described as doing in 1 Thessalonians 4:17 NKJ - **17** Then we who are alive *and* remain shall be caught up together with them in the clouds to meet the Lord in the air. And thus we shall always be with the Lord. They will not be left to struggle alone. The 144,000 of the bride plus the innumerable multitude are there to help them and council them along the way.

God is about justice, mercy and faith. God has a plan and a system that will not fail.

Matthew 23:23 NKJ - **23 (Jesus said), Woe to you, scribes and Pharisees, hypocrites! For you pay tithe of mint and anise and cummin, and have neglected the weightier *matters* of the law: justice and mercy and faith. These you ought to have done, without leaving the others undone.**

God says that ultimately according to His plan all will be saved, 2 Peter 3:9 NKJ - **9** The Lord is not slack concerning *His* promise, as some count slackness, but is longsuffering toward us, not willing that any should perish but that all should come to repentance.

John 12:32 NKJ – (Jesus said), **32 And I, if I am lifted up from the earth, will draw all *peoples* to Myself."**

"**All**" means everyone, everywhere with no exceptions.

From the millennium going forward into the future into the ages to come, world without end, death will not exist.

Everyone will live in the flesh until they become worthy of immortality then they will be changed to immortal as previously stated.

The plan God has in mind for humanity as described in the Bible is nothing close to what is being taught in the churches of this world. Ultimately the reward of the saved is to become a spirit born child of God and live in His family circle on and on and on with no end to life, ever...

CHAPTER TWENTY THREE
ANCIENT ISRAEL RESURRECTION

(The only exception to "no more death" will be those with Satan, who are Gog and Magog when Satan is loosed for a little season after the millennium.) Revelation 20:7 thru 9 NKJ - **7** Now when the thousand years have expired, Satan will be released from his prison **8** and will go out to deceive the nations which are in the four corners of the earth, Gog and Magog, to gather them together to battle, whose number *is* as the sand of the sea. **9** They went up on the breadth of the earth and surrounded the camp of the saints and the beloved city. And fire came down from God out of heaven and devoured them.

It is now time for the great dry bones resurrection to take place but who are these people? Ezekiel 37:11 NKJ - **11** Then He said to me, "Son of man, these bones are the whole house of Israel. They indeed say, 'Our bones are dry, our hope is lost, and we ourselves are cut off!'

The whole house of Israel or they are sometimes called the whole house of Jacob will come up in the second resurrection. There is no way to calculate how many people will be in this resurrection but it will number into the billions. There are billions of them alive in this generation.

Where will all of these resurrected people be taken to? Ezekiel 37:12 thru 14 NKJ - **12** Therefore prophesy and say to them, 'Thus says the Lord GOD: "Behold, O My people, I will open your graves and cause you to come up from your graves, and bring you into the <u>land of Israel</u>. **13** Then you shall know that I *am* the LORD, when I have opened your graves, O My people, and brought you up from your graves. **14** I will put My Spirit in you, and you shall live, and I will place you in your own land. Then you shall know that I, the LORD, have spoken *it* and performed *it,*" says the LORD.' "

No doubt the borders of Israel will be enlarged to accommodate this many resurrected humans; needing food and shelter.

We know already the topography of the earth will be changed <u>before</u> the millennium starts, the mountains are shaken down, the islands disappear and there is no more sea as written in Revelation 21:1 NKJ - **1** Now I saw a new heaven and a new earth, for the first heaven and the first earth had passed away. Also there was no more sea.

Ezekiel 39:7, 8 NKJ - **7** So I will make My holy name known in the midst of My people Israel, and I will not *let them* profane My holy name anymore. Then the nations shall know that *I am* the LORD, the Holy One in Israel. **8** Surely it is coming, and it shall be done," says the Lord GOD. "This *is* the day of which I have spoken.

Apparently during the millennium the earth is being prepared for this resurrection of the Great Last Day.

One can easily imagine the earth, especially that area of it to be occupied by the New Israel, to be as beautiful as a well-manicured golf course at the beginning of the millennium and it will be maintained as the millennium progresses.

CHAPTER TWENTY FOUR
IMPORTANT CHRISTIAN THINGS THAT REALLY MATTER

This biblical truth is not only shocking but it is beyond the scope of all belief and reason to people who have been raised from childhood only on Church doctrines that are mainly preconceived ideas of men. Men have come through thousands of pages of pagan theology passed off as Christian learning over hundreds of years.

We live in a society that has been badly deceived. Let's review some of what we have learned, things we have already brought to light before we continue.

People have been taught they have a soul, but the Bible tells us we are a soul. Then if we are good our soul will go to heaven and if we are bad our soul will go to hell when they die and be tormented forever in a lake of fire. The Bible does not say that!

Catholics are taught erroneously that they could possibly become strung out half way in between heaven and hell at a place they call purgatory if they are not bad enough for hell and not good enough for heaven. This is not a teaching from the Bible.

Church folks today for the most part are believing that the first day of the week is the Sabbath in clear defiance of God's word, the Holy Bible.

Genesis 2:1 thru 3 NKJ - **1** Thus the heavens and the earth, and all the host of them, were finished. **2** And on the seventh day God ended His work which He had done, and He rested on the seventh day from all His work which He had done. **3** Then God blessed the seventh day and sanctified it, because in it He rested from all His work which God had created and made.

Mark 2:27,28 NKJ - **27** And He (Jesus) said to them, **"The Sabbath was made for man, and not man for the Sabbath. 28 Therefore the Son of Man is also Lord of the Sabbath."**

Exodus 31:13 thru 17 NKJ - **13** "Speak also to the children of Israel, saying: 'Surely My Sabbaths you shall keep, for it *is* a sign between Me and you throughout your generations, that *you* may know that I *am* the LORD who sanctifies you. **14** You shall keep the Sabbath, therefore, for *it is* holy to you. Everyone who profanes it shall surely be put to death; for whoever does *any* work on it, that person shall be cut off from among his people. **15** Work shall be done for six days, but the seventh *is* the Sabbath of rest, holy to the LORD. Whoever does *any* work on the Sabbath day, he shall surely be put to death. **16** Therefore the children of Israel shall keep the Sabbath, to observe the Sabbath throughout their generations *as* a perpetual covenant. **17** It *is* a sign between Me and the children of Israel forever; for *in* six days the LORD made the heavens and the earth, and on the seventh day He rested and was refreshed.' "

If we were to be so bold as to pose the question of "What is sin?" The answer is found in 1 John 3:4 NKJ - **4** Whoever commits sin also commits lawlessness, and sin is lawlessness.

The next question would be to ask "What is the penalty for sin?" Romans 6:23 NKJ - **23** For the wages of sin *is* death.

What if we were to ask what are the laws of God for if you consider the Ten Commandments to be laws?

Romans 3:20 NKJ - **20** Therefore by the deeds of the law no flesh will be justified in His sight, for by the law *is* the knowledge of sin. (The law tells us what sin is).

What is the fourth of the Ten Commandments? Exodus 20:8 thru 11 NKJ - **8** "Remember the Sabbath day, to keep it holy. **9** Six days you shall labor and do all your work, **10** but the seventh day *is* the Sabbath of the Lord your God. *In it* you shall do no work: you, nor your son, nor your daughter, nor your male servant, nor your female servant, nor your cattle, nor your stranger who *is* within your gates. **11** For *in* six days the Lord made the heavens and the earth, the sea, and all that *is* in them, and rested the seventh day. Therefore the Lord blessed the Sabbath day and hallowed it.

HOLY DAYS

Not many churches today are observing the Christian Passover as Jesus and His disciples did. John 13:5 thru 15 NKJ - **5** After that, He (Jesus) poured water into a basin and began to wash the disciples' feet, and to wipe *them* with the towel with which He was girded. **6** Then He came to Simon Peter. And *Peter* said to Him, "Lord, are You washing my feet?" **7** Jesus answered and said to him, **"What I am doing you do not understand now, but you will know after this."** **8** Peter said to Him, "You shall never wash my feet!" Jesus answered him, **"If I do not wash you, you have no part with Me."** **9** Simon Peter said to Him, "Lord, not my feet only, but also *my* hands and *my* head!" **10** Jesus said to him, **"He who is bathed needs only to wash *his* feet, but is completely clean; and you are clean, but not all of you."** **11** For He knew who would betray Him; therefore He said, **"You are not all clean."** **12** So when He had washed their feet, taken His garments, and sat down again, He said to them, **"Do you know what I have done to you? 13 You call me Teacher and Lord, and you say well, for *so* I am. 14 If I then, *your* Lord and Teacher, have washed your feet, you also ought to wash one another's feet. 15 For I have given you an example, that you should do as I have done to you.**

Mark 14:22 thru 25 NKJ - **22** And as they were eating, Jesus took bread, blessed and broke *it,* and gave *it* to them and said, **"Take, eat; this is My body."** **23** Then He took the cup, and when He had given thanks He gave *it* to them, and they all drank from it. **24 And He said to them, "This is My blood of the new covenant, which is shed for many. 25 Assuredly, I say to you, I will no longer drink of the fruit of the vine until that day when I drink it new in the kingdom of God."**

People today observe a eucharist or they may call it the Lord's Supper, again in clear defiance of Paul's instruction to the Church at Corinth where they had gathered to keep the Passover. I Corinthians 11:20 NKJ - **20** Therefore when you come together in one place, it is not to eat the Lord's Supper. Only unleavened bread and wine were to be brought to the Passover service, they were not supposed to be eating a meal.

Jesus and His disciples did eat a meal together on their last gathering for Passover. It was Jesus as the Lord God of the Old Testament who instituted the first Passover in Egypt with a meal and the unleavened bread.

However, that night as Jesus was conducting the last Passover of the Old Testament with His disciples, it was the Old Covenant traditional Passover meal; Jesus introduced them to the sacraments of the New Covenant Passover; after they finished the Old Covenant Passover meal.

Jesus was to be the Passover lamb sacrificed for the sins of the world. The broken unleavened bread was a symbol of His body to be broken by a severe beating and the wine symbolized His blood to be spilled on the ground.

After this last Old Testament Passover meal the disciples no longer observed Passover with a meal. They washed feet and had broken unleavened bread and wine.

Today people are prone to use white leavened bread or a wafer and unfermented grape juice in the ceremony they call the "Lord's Supper" which the Apostle Paul admonished Christians not to do.

When it comes to holidays this is another misnomer. When God settled ancient Israel into their land He gave them certain days He pronounced as Holy Days on which the people were to assemble to worship Him. These were termed annual Sabbaths when no work was to be done.

God originally had established a priesthood from the descendants of Aaron who was a Levite like his brother Moses. It was called the Levitical Priesthood. Only Levites could serve in the priesthood and do the sacrifices.

The third book of the Bible is titled Leviticus which centers around the concept of the holiness of God and how an unholy people can acceptably approach Him and then remain in continued fellowship. In Leviticus 23:1 thru 3 NKJ - **1** And the Lord spoke to Moses, saying, **2** "Speak to the children of Israel, and say to them: 'The feasts of the Lord, which you shall proclaim *to be* holy convocations, these *are* My feasts.

3 'Six days shall work be done, but the seventh day *is* a Sabbath of solemn rest, a holy convocation. You shall do no work *on it;* it *is* the Sabbath of the LORD in all your dwellings. (God specified His weekly Sabbath).

Next God states the following to be the "Feasts of the Lord" all of which are Holy Days and Annual Sabbaths on which the people were to assemble for worship and no work was to be done. Leviticus 23:4 NKJ - **4** 'These *are* the feasts of the LORD, holy convocations which you shall proclaim at their appointed times.

In verses 5 thru 8 God lays out the Passover and days of unleavened bread. **5** On the fourteenth *day* of the first month at twilight *is* the LORD'S Passover. **6** And on the fifteenth day of the same month *is* the Feast of Unleavened Bread to the LORD; seven days you must eat unleavened bread. **7** On the first day you shall have a holy convocation; you shall do no customary work on it. **8** But you shall offer an offering made by fire to the LORD for seven days. The seventh day *shall be* a holy convocation; you shall do no customary work *on it.*' "

This was a fore runner picturing the sacrifice of Christ to come in the future.

In verses 9 thru 14 God commissioned the feast of the firstfruits which was the barley harvest. This was picturing Jesus Christ as the first human to be resurrected to a spirit being, the firstfruit or the first born of many brethren. This is what "born again" means.

All people will enter immortality through this procedure: death, burial and resurrection - **9** And the LORD spoke to Moses, saying, **10** "Speak to the children of Israel, and say to them: 'When you come into the land which I give to you, and reap its harvest, then you shall bring a sheaf of the firstfruits of your harvest to the priest. **11** He shall wave the sheaf before the LORD, to be accepted on your behalf; on the day after the Sabbath the priest shall wave it. **12** And you shall offer on that day, when you wave the sheaf, a male lamb of the first year, without blemish, as a burnt offering to the LORD. **13** Its grain offering *shall be* two-tenths *of an ephah* of fine flour mixed with oil, an offering made by fire to the LORD, for a sweet aroma; and its drink offering *shall be* of wine, one-fourth of a hin. **14** You shall eat neither bread nor parched grain nor fresh grain until the same day that you have brought an offering to your God; *it shall be* a statute forever throughout your generations in all your dwellings.

Next God commissioned the feast of Pentecost. This was the early harvest at the beginning of summer. It was the wheat harvest representing the first resurrection and the church being the spiritual harvest. **15** 'And you shall count for yourselves from the day after the Sabbath, from the day that you brought the sheaf of the wave offering: seven Sabbaths shall be completed. **16** Count fifty days to the day after the seventh Sabbath; then you shall offer a new grain offering to the LORD. **17** You shall bring from your dwellings two wave *loaves* of two-tenths *of an ephah.* They shall be of fine flour; they shall be baked with leaven. *They are* the firstfruits to the LORD. **18** And you shall offer with the bread seven lambs of the first year, without blemish, one young bull, and two rams. They shall be *as* a burnt offering to the LORD, with their grain offering and their drink offerings, an offering made by fire for a sweet aroma to the LORD. **19** Then you shall sacrifice one kid of the goats as a sin offering, and two male lambs of the first year as a sacrifice of a peace offering. **20** The priest shall wave them with the bread of the firstfruits *as* a wave offering before the LORD, with the two lambs. They shall be holy to the LORD for the priest. **21** And you shall proclaim on the same day *that* it is a holy convocation to you. You shall do no customary work *on it. It shall be* a statute forever in all your dwellings throughout your generations. **22** 'When you reap the harvest of your land, you shall not wholly reap the corners of your field when you reap, nor shall you gather any gleaning from your harvest. You shall leave them for the poor and for the stranger: I *am* the LORD your God.' "

The next Holy Day was not a feast it was a memorial of blowing of trumpets a warning of war.

Matthew 24:6 NKJ – (Jesus said), **6 And you will hear of wars and rumors of wars. See that you are not troubled; for all *these things* must come to pass, but the end is not yet.**

Leviticus 23:23 thru 25 NKJ - **23** Then the LORD spoke to Moses, saying, **24** "Speak to the children of Israel, saying: 'In the seventh month, on the first *day* of the month, you shall have a sabbath-*rest,* a memorial of blowing of trumpets, a holy convocation. **25** You shall do no customary work *on it;* and you shall offer an offering made by fire to the LORD.' "

The next Holy Day is the Day of Atonement. It is a day of fasting. It pictures the removal of Satan and peace coming to the earth for the first time since Adam was created, tempted and deceived.

Leviticus 23:26 thru 32 NKJ - **26** And the LORD spoke to Moses, saying: **27** "Also the tenth *day* of this seventh month *shall be* the Day of Atonement. It shall be a holy convocation for you; you shall afflict your souls, and offer an offering made by fire to the LORD. **28** And you shall do no work on that same day, for it *is* the Day of Atonement, to make atonement for you before the LORD your God. **29** For any person who is not afflicted *in soul* on that same day shall be cut off from his people. **30** And any person who does any work on that same day, that person I will destroy from among his people. **31** You shall do no manner of work; *it shall be* a statute forever throughout your generations in all your dwellings. **32** It *shall be* to you a sabbath of *solemn* rest, and you shall afflict your souls; on the ninth *day* of the month at evening, from evening to evening, you shall celebrate your sabbath."

Then comes the Feast of Tabernacles which is picturing the millennium. One thousand years of peace on earth while God is growing a new Israel. King David will be resurrected and ruling the New Israel, Jesus Christ will be here ruling the earth as King of Kings. The Apostles will be sitting on thrones judging the twelve tribes of Israel.

Leviticus 23:33 thru 38 NKJ - **33** Then the L ORD spoke to Moses, saying, **34** "Speak to the children of Israel, saying: 'The fifteenth day of this seventh month *shall be* the Feast of Tabernacles *for* seven days to the L ORD. **35** On the first day *there shall be* a holy convocation. You shall do no customary work *on it.* **36** *For* seven days you shall offer an offering made by fire to the L ORD. On the eighth day you shall have a holy convocation, and you shall offer an offering made by fire to the L ORD. It *is* a sacred assembly, *and* you shall do no customary work *on it.* **37** These *are* the feasts of the L ORD which you shall proclaim *to be* holy convocations, to offer an offering made by fire to the L ORD, a burnt offering and a grain offering, a sacrifice and drink offerings, everything on its day-- **38** besides the Sabbaths of the L ORD, besides your gifts, besides all your vows, and besides all your freewill offerings which you give to the L ORD.

After the millennium the Holy City New Jerusalem will be on earth. By some accounts it is 1377 miles square and high. All of the "saints" will have been given immortality at that time and the earth is positioned and ready for the resurrection of Ezekiel 37.

Then comes the Great Last Day. The last Holy Day of the year picturing post millennial earth and what lies beyond.

Leviticus 23:39, 44 NKJ - **39** 'Also on the fifteenth day of the seventh month, when you have gathered in the fruit of the land, you shall keep the feast of the L ORD *for* seven days; on the first day *there shall be* a sabbath-*rest,* and on the eighth day a sabbath-*rest.*

44 So Moses declared to the children of Israel the feasts of the LORD.

It is very possible that the great Last Day is a never ending day based on several things. God has moved His headquarters here upon the earth. Revelation 21:2,3 NKJ - **2** Then I, John, saw the holy city, New Jerusalem, coming down out of heaven from God, prepared as a bride adorned for her husband. **3** And I heard a loud voice from heaven saying, "Behold, the tabernacle of God *is* with men, and He will dwell with them, and they shall be His people. God Himself will be with them *and be* their God.

HOLY DAYS OR HOLIDAYS

We made a list of God's Holy Days but what do we find in our world today? We find in our country instead of the Passover, as instructed by God, we see Easter being celebrated in the spring. The Roman Catholic Church took a pagan celebration to the sun goddess "Ishtar" or Astarte", goddess of fertility, and sanctioned it to become a so called Christian holiday.

What do baby chicks, ducks, and bunny rabbits have to do with Jesus Christ and His sacrifice on the cross for the remission of our sins? These are symbols of fertility and an enticement to draw little children into the celebration of a pagan goddess falsely calling it a Christian holiday.

It does not take a genius to imagine that God is not pleased with such deceptive customs. People always start with the children by enticing them and drawing them into the holidays with gifts, new clothes, candy such as chocolate eggs and bunnies.

In December the children are again drawn into a pagan celebration called Christmas, they receive gifts, new clothes, candy etcetera.

Christmas has no connection with the birth of Christ, it is the most blatant manufactured holiday of all.

Going by our Gregorian calendar Jesus was born in late September, possibly on the 29th at the time people were coming to Jerusalem for the Feast of Tabernacles in 4 B.C. This explains the reason why no accommodations were available in Bethlehem. There were hundreds of people traveling toward Jerusalem from every corner of Israel and especially Judah.

Zechariah 14:19 NKJ - **19** This shall be the punishment of Egypt and the punishment of all the nations that do not come up to keep the Feast of Tabernacles.

The shepherds were out in the fields with their flocks. This is another clue that Christ was not born in the cold winter months. The shepherds always brought their flocks in from the fields by mid-October.

In the fourth century the Roman Catholic Church started the "Mass of Christ". This Church substituted the Son of God for the pagan sun god Saturnalia which was held on December 17th to the god Saturn.

The Roman Catholic Church moved the date from December 17th to December 25th to combine all of the pagan customs into one big celebration called the "Mass of Christ" or "Christ Mass" later shortened to Christmas. Why did the Roman Catholic Church make these changes and compromise with these pagans? The Emperor and the Pope had ordered the Catholic Church to do so.

The pagans all held a new year celebration to "SOL" their sun god. To them the old sun god died on the shortest day of the year and the new sun god arrived on the first day of each new year.

Saturnalia had been an unrestrained, extravagant, licentious, orgiastic celebration. Many secular people today celebrate Christmas in a very similar fashion.

When the question comes to mind, what do we do? We have to decide to observe God's Holy Days or the pagan Catholic holidays that are falsely called Christian.

It is important to God for us to consider a couple very pointed straight forward scriptures: Deuteronomy 12:32 NKJ - **32** Whatever I command you, be careful to observe it; you shall not add to it nor take away from it. Amos 5:21 NKJ - **21** "I hate, I despise your feast days, and I do not savor your sacred assemblies.

Jeremiah 10:1 thru 5 NKJ - **1** Hear the word which the LORD speaks to you, O house of Israel. **2** Thus says the LORD: "Do not learn the way of the Heathen; Do not be dismayed at the signs of heaven, for the Gentiles are dismayed at them. **3** For the customs of the peoples *are* futile; for *one* cuts a tree from the forest, the work of the hands of the workman, with the ax. **4** They decorate it with silver and gold; they fasten it with nails and hammers so that it will not topple. **5** They *are* upright, like a palm tree, and they cannot speak; they must be carried, because they cannot go *by themselves.* Do not be afraid of them, for they cannot do evil, nor can they do any good."

CHAPTER TWENTY FIVE
THE PARADISE OF GOD

Ezekiel 47:1,11,12 NKJ - **1** Then he brought me back to the door of the temple; and there was water, flowing from under the threshold of the temple toward the east, for the front of the temple faced east; the water was flowing from under the right side of the temple, south of the altar. **11** But its swamps and marshes will not be healed; they will be given over to salt. **12** Along the bank of the river, on this side and that, will grow all *kinds of* trees used for food; their leaves will not wither, and their fruit will not fail. They will bear fruit every month, because their water flows from the sanctuary. Their fruit will be for food, and their leaves for medicine."

Under the threshold of the temple, there is a stream flowing that becomes a river and flows down to the Dead Sea (salt sea) and it will overflow.

Ezekiel 47:9 thru 12 NKJ - **9** And it shall be *that* every living thing that moves, wherever the rivers go, will live. There will be a very great multitude of fish, because these waters go there; for they will be healed, and everything will live wherever the river goes. **10** It shall be *that* fishermen will stand by it from En Gedi to En Eglaim; they will be *places* for spreading their nets. Their fish will be of the same kinds as the fish of the Great Sea, exceedingly many. **11** But its swamps and marshes will not be healed; they will be given over to salt.

Notice carefully verse 12: **12** Along the bank of the river, on this side and that, will grow all *kinds of* trees used for food; their leaves will not wither, and their fruit will not fail. They will bear fruit every month, because their water flows from the sanctuary. Their fruit will be for food, and their leaves for medicine."

Revelation 22:2 NKJ - **2** In the middle of its street, and on either side of the river, *was* the tree of life, which bore twelve fruits, each *tree* yielding its fruit every month. The leaves of the tree *were* for the healing of the nations.

Notice here that the leaves are for the healing of the nations and in Ezekiel 47:12 they are for medicine.

We point this out because many people of today believe all human life will be over after the resurrection of Ancient Israel when they are converted and changed to spirit.

There is no biblical record of angels or spirit beings getting sick or needing medicine for healing which is a strong argument for the continuation of human life on planet earth to go on and on, life without end as written in Revelation 21:4 NKJ - **4** And God will wipe away every tear from their eyes; there shall be no more death, nor sorrow, nor crying. There shall be no more pain, for the former things have passed away."

This points to people living until they prove they are worthy to be trusted with immortality, then when they are thusly judged worthy they will be changed through the process of a metamorphosis such as we saw in 1 Thessalonians 4:17 NKJ - **17** Then we who are alive *and* remain shall be caught up together with them in the clouds to meet the Lord in the air. And thus we shall always be with the Lord.

The tree of life went out of existence in Genesis chapters 2 and 3. The tree of life will return and grow on the banks of the river of life which will be there from the beginning of the millennium onward, apparently forever.

In Revelation 2:7 NKJ – (Jesus said), **7 He who has an ear, let him hear what the Spirit says to the churches. To him who overcomes I will give to eat from the tree of life, which is in the midst of the Paradise of God." '**

We read that the tree of life is mentioned as being in the Paradise of God. The holy city, New Jerusalem is where the headquarters of the Paradise of God is located.

The tree of life will be growing there by the side of the river of life and there will be no more death. It truly is the Paradise of God and He will continue to grow His family on into the future world without end.

The human beings born during that time will become "born again" through a process of metamorphosis and become spirit beings they will not die.

God will continue to grow His family forever and we are not told if we will eventually go into space and develop new planets to support life by giving them favorable climates, oxygen, water and air.

God is so far ahead of us in His planning that it is mind boggling to try to imagine all He has in store for us and our future that will never end.

One thing we can count on is we will not be sitting around twiddling our thumbs. God is a planner, an inventor, an implementer and He is a delegator; so we will all be busy doing our assigned duties.

Another thing we can count on is that in a world with no Satan everything will be handled as God instructed; no one will be tearing down behind us.

Scriptures are just as true today as they were in the Old Testament time; some folks no doubt would take the position that the following scriptures all came from the Old Testament therefore they would have little or no bearing on Christ or the New Testament.

This is very dangerous reasoning for God is God and what He has declared will be. Also what He has commanded will be carried out in due time.

Malachi 3:6 NKJ - **6** "For I *am* the LORD, I do not change; therefore you are not consumed, O sons of Jacob.

Matthew 7:26 NKJ – (Jesus said) **26 But everyone who hears these sayings of Mine, and does not**

do them, will be like a foolish man who built his house on the sand.

Micah 6:8 NKJ - **8** He has shown you, O man, what *is* good; and what does the L ORD require of you but to do justly, to love mercy, and to walk humbly with your God?

The nation of Israel used to be the "people of God"; today Christians assume that privileged status. However it is the same God with the same rules and the same laws, God does not change; He is not wishy-washy.

Hebrews 13:8,9 NKJ - **8** Jesus Christ *is* the same yesterday, today, and forever. **9** Do not be carried about with various and strange doctrines.

Those who claim to be people of God which is much of this whole nation, facing the many problems we are having we should be constantly reminding ourselves of 2 Chronicles 7:14 NKJ - **14** If My people who are called by My name will humble themselves, and pray and seek My face, and turn from their wicked ways, then I will hear from heaven, and will forgive their sin and heal their land.

There is a good reason why we should pray for our leaders because a biblical principle is truth: "When a king rules justly the people prosper along with the country".

As we go along from day to day our mind should be on the future and what President Kennedy said in one of his speeches. "Ask not what your country can do for you, rather ask what you can do for your country."

We should go beyond that thought said years ago and reach out by encouraging others, physically, mentally, and spiritually, and begin our mode toward something important that really matters. Jesus said, "Love your neighbor as yourself".

CHAPTER TWENTY SIX
CONCLUSION

There are no more important things in life than those pertaining to the spiritual side of our existence.

There are plenty of books that have been written on the secular side of life such as education, finance, all kinds of self-help books for example: health manuals, beauty tips, politics and government. All of that does matter but the two big questions must be addressed which is: what is the final answer and what is the real truth?

The one best seller book that has been written to guide humanity safely through life from the cradle to the grave and beyond is the Holy Bible.

Our country began by making the Holy Bible required reading in schools from grade school to graduation and many homes were blessed to have a Bible; most of the homes did have a family Bible.

Today in the year 2016, our country has invoked the view that public education should be conducted without the introduction of God in the class room; they have gone secular; a horrendous mistake!

The education system has gone secular toward the Bible but not to the Qu'ran. The Qu'ran is the book of Satan, it has allowed Satan to win temporarily.

Today's children will grow up with a skewed view of Who and What God is about because of this pagan religion being allowed in our schools, Satan is taking over.

We have had a Muslim sympathizer in the White House for two terms and just look at the condition of our country. Prosperity has been rapidly leaving our shores; we will soon be on a level with the third world countries if this trend continues. God is not pleased!

My question to my fellow Americans is this, "Why do you believe what you believe religiously, politically, health wise and otherwise? Is your vision cock-eyed? These questions are the most important since we are all responsible for our future individually and together as a nation.

It is good to know that our future and our salvation is at stake as well as the future of our country. Our country will not survive as a secular Godless society with special interest groups and greed they will finish tearing everything apart. Remember the words of Nathan Hale, "If we don't hang together we will all hang separately"!

To continue as a nation we must join together, put our trust and confidence in our Creator and realize that He has set apart all who are righteous. To be fore warned is to be fore armed.

If every class in every school in the U.S.A. would require every student in every grade to recite the first fourteen verses of Deuteronomy every morning when class convenes we would see a difference in the society by the next generation. These words would be forever in their conscience.

Deuteronomy 28:1 thru 4 NKJ - **1** "Now it shall come to pass, if you diligently obey the voice of the LORD your God, to observe carefully all His commandments which I command you today, that the LORD your God will set you high above all nations of the earth. **2** And all these blessings shall come upon you and overtake you, because you obey the voice of the LORD your God: **3** Blessed *shall* you *be* in the city, and blessed *shall* you *be* in the country. **4** Blessed *shall be* the fruit of your body, the produce of your ground and the increase of your herds, the increase of your cattle and the offspring of your flocks. **5** Blessed *shall be* your basket and your kneading bowl. **6** Blessed *shall* you *be* when you come in, and blessed *shall* you *be* when you go out. **7** "The LORD will cause your enemies who rise against you to be defeated before your face; they shall come out against you one way and flee before you seven ways. **8** The LORD will command the blessing on you in your storehouses and in all to which you set your hand, and He will bless you in the land which the LORD your God is giving you. **9** The LORD will establish you as a holy people to Himself, just as He has sworn to you, if you keep the commandments of the LORD your God and walk in His ways. **10** Then all peoples of the earth shall see that you are called by the name of the LORD, and they shall be afraid of you. **11** And the LORD will grant you plenty of goods, in the fruit of your body, in the increase of your livestock, and in the produce of your ground, in the land of which the LORD swore to your fathers to give you. **12** The LORD will open to you His good treasure, the heavens, to give the rain to your land in its season, and to bless all the work of your hand. You shall lend to many nations, but you shall not borrow. **13** And the LORD will make you the head and not the tail; you shall be above only, and not be beneath, if you heed the commandments of the LORD your God, which I command you today, and are careful to observe *them.* **14** So you shall not turn aside from any of the words which I command you this day, *to* the right or the left, to go after other gods to serve them.

When we sing the song "God Bless America", keep in mind, that request is not likely to be honored if we are not obedient to Him. God has always turned His back to disobedient and gainsaying people, but He is quick to respond to the requests of the obedient.

It is painfully evident today that not many children are being drilled on these living promises mentioned in Deuteronomy nor are our children even being exposed to them at home or at school.

These are pure basic training instructions every child should have as they can set their life goals to ensure peace, happiness and prosperity and to respect each other.

Just blundering through life learning from our mistakes, not knowing where the path we take will lead us would not be a good way to go.

A wise and caring parent will do their utmost to give their children a rock solid foundation and a good education, both secular and religious (spiritual) education to help them attain a balanced successful life.